WILMETTE PUBLIC LIBRARY

3 1239 00822 2561

P9-CRB-014

THANK
&
GROW
RICH

WITHDRAWN
Wilmette Public Library

Wilmette Public Library
1242 Wilmette Ave.
Wilmette, IL 60091
847-256-5025

ALSO BY PAM GROUT

Books

Jumpstart Your Metabolism:
How to Lose Weight by Changing the Way You Breathe

Art and Soul: 156 Ways to Free Your Creative Spirit

Living Big: Embrace Your Passion and
Leap into an Extraordinary Life

Kansas Curiosities: Quirky Characters,
Roadside Oddities & Other Offbeat Stuff

Colorado Curiosities: Quirky Characters,
Roadside Oddities & Other Offbeat Stuff

Girlfriend Getaways: You Go Girl! And I'll Go, Too

You Know You're in Kansas When: 101 Quintessential Places,
People, Events, Customs, Lingo, and Eats of the Sunflower State

Recycle This Book: And 72½ Even
Better Ways to Save "Yo Momma" Earth

God Doesn't Have Bad Hair Days: Ten Spiritual Experiments
That Will Bring More Abundance, Joy, and Love to Your Life

The 100 Best Vacations to Enrich Your Life

The 100 Best Worldwide Vacations to Enrich Your Life

The 100 Best Volunteer Vacations to Enrich Your Life

E-Squared: Nine Do-It-Yourself Energy Experiments That Prove Your
Thoughts Create Your Reality (also available as an audio book)*

E-Cubed: Nine More Energy Experiments That Prove Manifesting
Magic and Miracles Is Your Full-Time Gig
(also available as an audio book)*

Card Deck

The Oracle of E: A 52-card Deck and Guidebook
to Manifest Your Dreams (with Colette Baron-Reid)*

*Available from Hay House
Please visit:

Hay House USA: www.hayhouse.com®
Hay House Australia: www.hayhouse.com.au
Hay House UK: www.hayhouse.co.uk
Hay House South Africa: www.hayhouse.co.za
Hay House India: www.hayhouse.co.in

THANK
&
GROW
RICH

A 30-Day Experiment in Shameless Gratitude and Unabashed Joy

PAM GROUT

WILMETTE PUBLIC LIBRARY

HAY HOUSE, INC.
Carlsbad, California • New York City
London • Sydney • Johannesburg
Vancouver • New Delhi

Copyright © 2016 by Pam Grout

Published and distributed in the United States by: Hay House, Inc.: www.hayhouse.com® • *Published and distributed in Australia by:* Hay House Australia Pty. Ltd.: www.hayhouse.com.au • *Published and distributed in the United Kingdom by:* Hay House UK, Ltd.: www.hayhouse.co.uk • *Published and distributed in the Republic of South Africa by:* Hay House SA (Pty), Ltd.: www.hayhouse.co.za • *Distributed in Canada by:* Raincoast Books: www.raincoast.com • *Published in India by:* Hay House Publishers India: www.hayhouse.co.in

Cover design: Amy Rose Grigoriou • *Interior design:* Pamela Homan

All rights reserved. No part of this book may be reproduced by any mechanical, photographic, or electronic process, or in the form of a phonographic recording; nor may it be stored in a retrieval system, transmitted, or otherwise be copied for public or private use—other than for "fair use" as brief quotations embodied in articles and reviews—without prior written permission of the publisher.

The author of this book does not dispense medical advice or prescribe the use of any technique as a form of treatment for physical, emotional, or medical problems without the advice of a physician, either directly or indirectly. The intent of the author is only to offer information of a general nature to help you in your quest for emotional and spiritual well-being. In the event you use any of the information in this book for yourself, the author and the publisher assume no responsibility for your actions.

Cataloging-in-Publication Data is on file with the
Library of Congress

Tradepaper ISBN: 978-1-4019-4984-6
Digital ISBN: 978-1-4019-4985-3

10 9 8 7 6 5 4 3 2
1st edition, August 2016

Printed in the United States of America

179.
9
GR

*This book is for everyone
who hears the dog whistle.
You know who you are.*

9/7/101

D-J

CONTENTS

"It is a sign of mediocrity to demonstrate gratitude with moderation."

— ROBERTO BENIGNI,
ACTOR, SCREENWRITER,
AND DIRECTOR

INTRODUCTION

"Life is a ticket to the greatest show on earth."
— MARTIN H. FISCHER, PHYSICIAN AND AUTHOR

In 2013, my world was choke-slammed upside down. And I mean that in the best possible way. After 20-plus years of being a writer, sitting in my pajamas penning 15 books and countless magazine articles, I dropped the tracks for *E-Squared*. For whatever reason (luck, timing, planets aligning), that little black book with the funny title shot up into the stratosphere, capturing the number one spot on the *New York Times* bestseller list. It has since been translated into 30-some languages.

To this day, I can't open my in-box without finding e-mails that start with some version of "You are never going to believe this."

It's like waking up every morning to my own self-help channel. "Guess what?" readers will write. "I just won $500," or "I just got my dream job on a horse farm." And I get to celebrate with them right here in Lawrence, Kansas. I get to add to their energy of excitement and joy.

I am deeply humbled to think my words might have helped even one person recognize a deeper truth. I am infinitely grateful that the do-it-yourself experiments in *E-Squared* cracked open a window to the unending benefi-cence of the universe.

In fact, if any serious researcher out there is looking for evidence that the world is limitless, abundant, and strangely accommodating—one of nine spiritual principles covered in *E-Squared*—I've got a whole folder full of lab report sheets I'd be willing to share.

Occasionally, however, I get an e-mail from a reader who's pissed. They want to know who I think I am, claiming the world is a beautiful place. They want to know why all the good stuff happens to everybody else. They claim to have seen no evidence of what I call the *field of infinite potentiality* (the "FP"), and they're going to, poor things, go out and eat worms.

This book is for them. And for that scared little place in all of us that still can't quite believe the universe actually likes us and works in cahoots with our highest aspirations.

When I can, I write back to these unhappy naysayers. I often send a blog post about my own days of worm cuisine. I encourage them to give it one more shot, to keep looking for the magic.

I started to notice a pattern within these anomalous "Why me?" letters. As I said, they sound a lot like my own crazy voices, the wild-haired loudmouths that still occasionally raise their hands in the back of my head.

"Hey, you!" they like to scream. "You're all alone. The world doesn't care about you. This is all bullshit."

Those voices are the popular kids. The ones who make the nightly news, the ones we discuss around the watercooler, the ones we appoint commissions and launch websites to fight. In other words, the dominant paradigm.

But they're not the truth. They will never be the truth.

Another theme I noticed is just how *hard* these readers are trying—repeating affirmations, making vision boards, drawing focus wheels.

I have nothing against those practices. I've been known to use some of them myself. But what happens when we fight and work and struggle, because we think nothing will change unless we do, is we put up roadblocks to all the good that wants to manifest right before our eyes.

The last thing I noticed about the "life sucks" e-mails is how deadly serious they all were. Oh! The gravitas! The sobriety!

"I did everything exactly as you said," they'd accuse with a hint of feral anger.

And every time, I was tempted to tell a stupid joke or make a goofball face. Anything to get them to—*lighten up, people!* The whole idea is to have fun! To play around in the quantum sandbox!

But yelling at serious people never works. At least it never works on the serious voices in my own head.

But here's what does: Giving myself a break. Counting my blessings. And getting on the frequency of joy and gratitude.

The Radio Transmitting Tower Known as You

> *"I can't just sit here vibrating with my own joy—*
> *I have to write about it, I have to share it."*
>
> — DAVID MASON, POET

Who can forget the explosive scene from the movie *A Few Good Men*? Tom Cruise has Jack Nicholson on the witness stand. Cruise is badgering him, wanting to know whether or not he ordered a Code Red.

Nicholson, getting redder and madder, finally erupts: "You can't handle the truth."

And that, in a nutshell, is the real answer to those e-mails wanting to know why all the good stuff happens to everyone else.

Until we can get on the frequency of gratitude, our connection to the bigger thing is blocked. Our bandwidth can't handle the eternal, infinite love of the Divine Broadcast that constantly airs possibility, joy, freedom. We've clogged up the connection by giving the floor to our inner anxieties, our fears, our time-sucking melodramas. Like Cinderella's stepsisters, we've crammed life's unending beneficence into our tiny shoes of old judgments and antiquated programming.

So in this book, we're going to upgrade the bandwidth of our consciousness. By using a simple, straightforward practice that takes at most five minutes a day, you will rewire your nervous system, rewrite old habits, and literally change the chemistry of your brain.

And that's where gratitude comes in.

Ode to Joy

> *"If your mind isn't cluttered by unnecessary things, this could be the best day of your life."*
>
> — FROM A MESSAGE LEFT ON MY VOICE MAIL
> BY THE ZING, AKA ETHAN HUGHES
> OF THE POSSIBILITY ALLIANCE

Gratitude?

Really?

Isn't that sort of, well, lame?

You just wrote a pair of powerhouse books about energy and infinite possibility. And now you're just gonna sell out and write about something pantywaist like gratitude? That's so basic, so flimsy, so 101 . . .

Hold on, Sparky.

The gratitude I'm talking about in this book is anything but flimsy or 101. Let's call it ferocious gratitude. In-your-face gratitude. None of the namby-pamby, sunshine-and-lollipops crap.

Because here's the thing. When we don't stop daily to inventory all the gazillion things going right in our lives, the crazy voices in our heads try to make us their bitch.

When we don't militantly count our blessings, the voices start jabbering, telling us that life sucks, that *we* suck. They're like the ticker crawl at the bottom of a news broadcast, running continuously in a nonstop loop.

As long as we keep tuning in to these voices, we fail to notice the incredible gift we've been given: to be here on planet Earth, to have this day, to enjoy this cosmic adventure. As long as we continue to etch their bald-faced lies deeper and deeper into our psyches, we cloud over our profound transformative connection to the field of infinite potentiality.

By simply stopping every day and registering our connection to this undeniable, unchanging Presence, we start to notice a deeper truth, a happier reality. We start to notice an eternal broadcast airing its joyful melody quietly beneath the static.

No offense to Napoleon Hill, the author of the self-help classic on which my title riffs, but the real power is in *not* thinking. If you want to override your brain's unfortunate habit of leafing through your past and creating a present hologram to match, *forget* thinking. And start thanking. And I mean thanking everything. The bills that are stacking up. The doctor's report you weren't expecting. The buffoon of a boyfriend who drank an entire bottle of tequila last night and puked on your new Oriental carpet.

When we practice this brand of ferocious gratitude— what I have dubbed the *extreme sport of gratitude*—we come to realize that all the striving, the endless struggle, the perpetual scrambling for our place in line, is unnecessary. In truth, it's counterproductive and actually blocks the energy field that is and always has been available to sustain and guide us.

Brazen gratitude provides a portal, an entry point straight into the heart of the very field of infinite possibilities my other two Hay House books introduced. It puts you on an energetic frequency, a vibration that calls in miracles.

When you're on this frequency (and it's *very* different from Eddie Haskell "That's a lovely dress, Mrs. Cleaver" platitudes), there's really very little else you have to do. The universe happily shows up with blessings and guidance. All you have to do is nod, don your scarf and new shades, and enjoy the ride.

Giving thanks, recognizing all the good in your life, is the gateway drug to a life most extraordinary. It's the superpower that moves you onto the frequency where beauty and joy and creativity happen.

And here's the big "secret." You don't have to work at connecting with this energy field. You don't have to be good enough to merit its attention. Or follow any formula to find it. You really don't have to do anything . . .

Except . . .

. . . quit listening to the voices. Quit creating static.

This sweet, loving, all-knowing energy force is here right now, waiting like the bull on the other side of the rodeo gate, ready to charge out the very second you lift the barriers of all you've been taught. It's pawing at the dirt, chomping at the bit, waiting for you to recognize that pretty much everything you've learned since the moment you popped out into the material plane is dead wrong.

This universal energy force never disappears. Or plays peekaboo or hide-and-go-seek. It never falters. It never does anything but love and give and bestow blessings.

This book is yet another chance (but please know you don't *need* this book or anything or anyone else) to prove there's a better way, a more natural way of living. It will help you tap into a frequency where miracles are as common as pie.

Like my previous Hay House books that offer real-time experiments, this one offers a 30-day trial in ferocious, militant, in-your-face gratitude. Spirituality, as I've always said, should be more than theory.

The hypothesis for the 30-day experiment is insanely simple: If you devote yourself to scouting blessings, you'll find them out the wazoo. If you turn each day into a 24-hour miracle reconnaissance mission, you'll call forth Truth. You'll get the happily ever after.

The book also contains 27 party games (who needs exercises?) that are easy to play, rip-roaringly fun, and guaranteed to build your abundance portfolio. (I'll talk more about the five components of this blue-chip capital in later chapters.)

Just know that by the time you have finished the month-long gratitude party prescribed in this book, you will look around at the parallel universe you've suddenly entered and think, *Really? Whatever happened to my depression? My fear? Was I insane back then?*

You will behold the proof, as *A Course in Miracles* promises, that love trumps fear, laughter trumps tears, and abundance trumps loss.

And it all starts with recognizing the beauty that surrounds you, flows through you, fills you with light. It all starts with getting on the frequency of gratitude.

PART I

LET THE GAMES BEGIN

*"You better have fun. Because
you're going to be gone in a minute."*

— JAMIE FOXX, ACTOR

1

FREQUENCY

"Listen silently and you can hear the frequency of love."
— JAROD KINTZ, AUTHOR
OF *THIS BOOK IS NOT FOR SALE*

I once carried an enormous cardboard box into Toast-masters. I asked my audience who would choose to spend an evening staring at it. They, quite rightly, thought I was crazy.

I then pointed out that watching TV is exactly that—staring at a box. What's interesting is not the box, but the electromagnetic radio waves (the frequency) that bring in pictures of, say, Leonard and Sheldon playing Rock, Paper, Scissors, Lizard, Spock.

When you look behind the scenes, even at things that look stable and uninterrupted, you find waves and particles shaking and shimmying, acting nothing like the solid image you think you see.

All matter—be it the Milky Way, a tomato, or the driveway on which the neighbor kid is chalking pastel dragons—is a frequency, a compilation of energy waves doubling as the Milky Way, a tomato, the driveway.

Even stuff you can't see is energy that by your command forms into a solid appearance.

But it's only that—an appearance. It's a hologram that looks astonishingly real because you trained your senses to see it that way.

According to Dr. Donald Hoffman, professor of cognitive science at University of California–Irvine, everything we think we see is a construction of the brain, a perceptual hack that hides the complexity of the real world.

The oak tree you "see" outside your window is mostly empty space and bouncing microscopic atoms. But by constructing a hologram of an oak tree, you create an interface, a simple tool to help you navigate information and pull what you need from the immeasurable field. Our brains are talented forgers, weaving a tapestry of meaning and perception so detailed and compelling that it never occurs to us to question it. The world you "see" reflects your dominant ideas, wishes, and emotions.

Take a close look at this paragraph:

```
<a     href="https://pamgrout.files.wordpress.
com/2009/07/bara-zip.jpg"><img     src="http://
pamgrout.files.wordpress.com/2009/07/bara-
zip.jpg?w=300"  alt="bara  zip"  width="600"
height="500" class="alignright size-medium wp-
image-7350" /></a>
```

Makes little sense, right? Unless you happen to know HTML (hypertext markup language), which creates what we see on our computers and phones. Drop it in your browser and it looks like this:

That's me zip-lining through the jungles of the Dominican Republic.

This is what happens in our minds. Like computers, we translate our personal HTML (a bunch of learned thoughts) into vibrations and pictures that show up in our hologram.

Rather than sort through the cacophony of energy waves—the uncountable possibilities out there in the universe—we pluck out a paltry few and name them "reality."

The FP, as I've nicknamed the field of infinite potentiality, works a little like the cloud in cyberspace, offering a shared pool of unlimited resources. We choose which ones to download, which ones to animate into our life experience.

Most of us simply download from "the FP cloud" the same possibilities, the same energy waves, as our parents, as our culture. Therefore, we create the same hologram, more or less, as our ancestors. Some of us have had the same preset button since we were five.

Everything we see in the material world starts as a wave of energy (also known as a thought) that eventually manifests as a solid-appearing object. When Steve Jobs and his engineers came up with the iPhone, it started as an idea, a thought, an energy wave that with their continued focus turned into a material object that, last I heard, 700 million of us have stuffed into our pockets.

And just like my iPhone has its own unique apps and contact lists, each of us download a particular energy field, a signature frequency. In this lifetime, for example, I've downloaded a tall female body that likes to write and travel and get nervous in front of large audiences.

This frequency goes out into the universe, transmitting our beliefs and expectations. This signal drives our lives, emanating a vibration that turns into invisible electromagnetic waves that attract situations and experiences that match.

Your vibration creates your subjective experience of life's ever-changing phenomena, schedules your lineup of coming attractions. You can use this powerful vibration to spot, analyze, and decipher problems. Or you can use it to livestream the mind of God.

Amp Up Your Frequency

> "Grow in happiness . . . and you'll glow in this
> peaceful way. Your friends will be very, very happy
> with you. Everyone will want to sit next to you.
> And people will give you money!"
>
> — DAVID LYNCH, FILMMAKER

When you get on the joy and gratitude frequency that I write about in this book, you radiate an energy that draws things into your life. The right people serendipitously walk across your path. The answer to a troubling question miraculously appears.

And while they can't quite put their finger on it, people notice.

"What's up with Joe?" they say. "There's something about him. Something . . . kinda odd. He's like—I don't know—unreasonably happy."

Being around such a person automatically lifts your spirits. It's not so much what they say or what they do. It's just this magical feeling you get from being in their presence.

Take Brother Lawrence, for example. Born Nicolas Herman, this Carmelite brother who worked in the kitchen of a Paris monastery back in the 1600s, was so radiant, so "I want what he's got," that people came from across Europe just to watch him peel potatoes. Can you imagine? A guy performing mundane chores becoming a spectator sport. That's the Divine Buzz, the natural state in action. Some of the bishops of his day reported that he lived in such profound peace and wonderment that he actually levitated.

In Spain, they call this energy *duende*. If you *tener* (have) *duende*, it means there's something invisible that draws magic your way. Spanish poet Federico García Lorca once described it as a fiery spirit, something that "climbs up inside you, from the soles of the feet."

There's no mistaking it when you're tuned in.

Life just works better.

I notice that when I'm on the joy and gratitude frequency, I'm a better writer, a better mother, a better pickleball player. Food tastes better, songs sound sweeter, and complete strangers send me love notes.

If you want to be a crazy strong electromagnet for love, be playful. Be astonished. Be grateful.

Only then can the universe and its divine explosion of possibilities get serious with you.

2

STATIC

"You can't be freaked out and
pissed off and expect to manifest."
— JAY PRYOR, MY FRIEND AND
FABULOUS EXECUTIVE LIFE COACH

"C'mon, Pam," people often say to me. "Living life with a party hat on seems irresponsible. If what you contend is true, why aren't more of us living in perpetual magic?"

Same reason we don't always get a clear signal on our TV or our cell phone drops a call. Our frequency is fuzzy. There's static. An energetic cloud blocks the universal flow of good. Sort of like Pigpen from the *Peanuts* cartoon.

The problem has never been reluctance on the part of the universe. The problem is our inability to see the beautiful, loving Truth it continually offers.

In my book *E-Squared*, I wrote about a woman who was so busy moaning and kvetching that she could not see the bus she was waiting for. The very thing she most wanted was invisible to her because she was on a frequency of pain and suffering.

A reader named Christine, after finishing that chapter, had one of those "Yeah, right!" reactions. Yet the following week, she experienced the same thing.

On her way to a bloggers' meet-up, she got frustrated when the pin on her iPhone failed to accurately guide her. She doubled back and forth in front of what was purportedly the address, getting madder and madder. Finally, she stopped, closed her eyes, took a deep breath, and opened her eyes—to see the building right in front of her.

"I had actually passed it three times," she says.

So if a disgruntled mood can make a bus and a building "disappear," can you imagine what else may be "invisible" when we stay on a grumpy frequency?

In June 2009, *The Journal of Neuroscience* published a study that proved when test subjects were on unhappy frequencies (I think scientists referred to this phenomenon as "in bad moods"), their visual cortexes—the part of the brain responsible for sight—were not able to properly process information. Happy test subjects found 50 percent more of what they were looking for than their unhappy counterparts.

You might have seen the "invisible gorilla" video posted on my blog: http://pamgrout.com/2013/09/23. The fact that more than half the viewers fail to see a big, hairy gorilla that walks through the center of the gym and beats its chest is pretty compelling evidence that we miss important things.

Thinking-Cap Defects

"Almost all humans have OCD of the mind."
— RICHARD ROHR, FRANCISCAN PRIEST

At this stage in our evolution, we humans have learned to over-rely on the tiny blob of plasma in our skulls that, quite frankly, is not logistically programmed to make dreams come true. It's programmed to see what it saw yesterday. To give you more of what you've already asked for. Like Google ads.

Every time I open my laptop, I get an ad hawking some version of the very thing I last googled. Right now, for example, I'm shopping for pickleball shoes. So even though I'm attempting to open a Wikipedia page, or Facebook, little ads pop up for sports shoes. Or if I'm planning a trip to, say, Los Angeles, I get pithy little sales pitches for hotels near LAX.

Your brain works the same way. It accesses the big cloud of possibility and says, "Well, she's looking for relationship drama. Let's send that," or "He's looking for money struggle; let's serve up a helping of overdue bills."

As *A Course in Miracles* repeats—again and again—we have replaced reality with our illusions. The first 50 lessons of the Course, in fact, train us to let go of any belief that what we see is objective fact.

What we see—all we see—is a hologram of past disgruntlements and fears.

Even though we believe our vision is like a camera, simply recording in real time all the shapes, objects, and motions we see, the truth is the brain's 130 million photoreceptors are joined by billions of neurons and synapses that construct and reconstruct literally anything our consciousness asks for.

Once we let go of our massively false beliefs about perception (that we're seeing something real), we open up to a lot of new possibilities. Reality, it turns out, is a lot more fascinating and unexpected than we ever imagined.

SDKCIRJTDHESIDIJFKFI

> *"The running commentary that dominates my field of consciousness is kind of an asshole."*
>
> — DAN HARRIS, ABC *NIGHTLINE* CO-ANCHOR

Like gravity, a person's energetic static isn't something we can really see, but it operates just as consistently. Grumpy thoughts, unhappy attitudes, and declarations that "life sucks" keep the world's goodness locked out. When we feel ornery, when we start tuning in to all the "problems" in our lives, we keep the world's channel of love and beneficence at bay. It's like the connection to the Divine is blinking on and then off again.

As long as we continue to hang on to old mental architecture that insists we must struggle and suffer and engage in complicated regimes (whether it be meditating or loving yourself or giving up gluten and sugar), we will be blind to all the gifts the universe offers up on a daily basis.

Let's do a short rundown of static's innumerable incarnations:

— **Our fundamental cultural paradigm.** From the get-go, we're taught that we are separate entities and, at our core, selfish and only out for ourselves.

To deal with this "problem," we are taught to rein in our impulses, to get ourselves under control. Our main "job" (and indeed *job* is a fitting description of our journey through life) is to seek out problems, compose plans to eliminate them, and use willpower to stay in line. The message that we must be coerced into doing "the right thing" is everywhere. Let's look at a few:

- Humans are careless. (*Don't speed or else you'll have to go to court and pay a fine.*)
- They're lazy. (*Workers need rules and supervisors.*)
- They're indolent. (*Without grades, students would never learn.*)

Even worse is how cruelly we reprimand ourselves, seduced by our own negative mantras: *I'm a failure. I'm bad. How could you?* we say to ourselves anytime we eat something we shouldn't, anytime we score less than perfect 10s on job evaluations, anytime we have a "bad-hair day." We're downright mean to ourselves. We go to war with those parts of ourselves we deem as unacceptable— the jiggly upper arms, the desire to dance in church, the pull we feel to skip work and write—and only end up crippling humanity as a whole.

The answers, we're taught, are:

Control. Discipline. Protection.

But willpower only separates us from our true nature, only creates static that keeps us from recognizing that we are part of something thrilling and unfathomable that may never have happened before in the entire galaxy and may never happen again.

— The maniac in our own heads. Waterboarding has nothing on the torture that sometimes takes place in my brain. A nonstop voice loop reminds me of all that's lacking in my life. This obnoxious voice (think Miss Trunchbull, the sadistic headmistress in Roald Dahl's *Matilda*) keeps tabs on all I'm doing wrong and makes long lists of things I need to improve.

It insists I should try really hard to "be a better person." Its ears perk up anytime someone mentions a new self-help book. It's for my own good, it says.

This voice is very clear that something is wrong with me. It tells me that, unlike everyone else, I have glaring flaws.

"Pam," it likes to say, "you don't quite measure up to other people, the cool people. You aren't as funny. Your skin's not as clear. And while you sometimes have a way with words, you're basically day-old Alpo compared to say Pat Conroy or Mary Karr. You might as well just get in bed and start tomorrow."

For the longest time, I thought this voice was *me*. It did a very convincing impersonation. I took the voice to therapy. I explained its opinions about my worth to my friends. I believed that when I voiced its concerns, I was voicing my concerns.

It wasn't until I began counting my blessings that the other frequency was able to make contact, the still, small one that whispered kind truths. *I* liked what it was saying. It suggested I start focusing on how deeply I am loved. How truly beautiful the world is.

It suggested the most important thing I could do for myself was get happy. Quit judging myself.

The Miss Trunchbull voice, it whispered gently, *is not you. It's a pseudo-Pam that you installed when you were very young, a voice that pretends to be you and pretends to be very, very important.*

The still, small voice reminded me that everything I see, everything I believe, is just a story I made up. It told me that, in Truth, I am spirit. I am light. All those voices, those wars going on in my head, are nothing but chunks of the collective consciousness that I can either believe and defend against or I can transmute with gratitude.

The real me, it told me, is kind, giving, in deep communion with all of creation. The real me is a true force for love.

— "It's not fair" and other patterns of thinking that lead us around by the nose. Anytime we look at a situation and feel that it should be other than it is, the malevolent puppeteer in our brain erects a wall of static.

Here are a few other plot points the evil puppeteer uses to heckle us:

- *Something needs to be fixed.*

- *There's only so much to go around.*

- *If I give of myself, people will take advantage.*

- *If I follow my heart, I'll be alone.*

- *If I pursue my passion, I'll be a laughingstock.*

- *It's dangerous to follow my joy.*

— Sloppy judgment. The minute you judge something (*This party isn't any fun; this drive is taking too long; this person is so boring*), you miss everything from that point on. Instead of Thoreau-ing our lives (sucking out the marrow), instead of carpe diem–ing our day, we squander most of its 1,440 moments wanting something else.

Why want the line to move faster, to be with different people, to be in a different situation? When right now, in this very moment, with these very people, in this exact situation, you can have everything you could ever want.

"Judge not" means more than refraining from judging others. It also means keeping your consciousness open.

Give Your Mind a New Job

> *"If you found yourself in paradise, it wouldn't be
> long before your mind would say, 'Yes, but . . . .'"*
>
> — ECKHART TOLLE, AUTHOR OF *THE POWER OF NOW*

Anyone who has tried to meditate or quiet the chatty little "asshat" in the mind knows it never disappears completely.

That's why, in this book, we're going to give it a brand-new assignment. An assignment that will keep it occupied just long enough for the kind, generous, eternal voice to have the floor.

By brazenly counting the innumberable things that are working in your life, you override the asshat and move right into the magic.

3

CHANGE YOUR FREQUENCY— CHANGE THE WORLD

"Somewhere, something incredible is waiting to be known."
— CARL SAGAN, ASTRONOMER

This is the chapter for the eye-rollers, the snickerers, the folks who think, *Gratitude is sweet and all, but there are rain forests to be saved. Starving children to feed.*

I would like to suggest that there is nothing more important you could ever do for yourself, your family, your friends, your planet, and, yes, even for the starving children than to tune in to the frequency of gratitude and joy.

The world right now is crying out for a team of "radio towers" who are beaming in the cosmic energy of infinite possibility. It needs a force of human frequencies who believe in the invisible power of light and love.

At every moment, whether you know it or not, you are contributing to the collective consciousness. Your thoughts, your energy field, your frequency is putting out an electromagnetic charge that either adds to the old story—the story of lack and limitation—or beams in the new story.

I think we can all agree we could use a new story.

The old story, the story of separation, tells us our thoughts, our beliefs, our energy fields . . . don't really matter, not in the vast universe of others. It tells us that force and control and taking action is the way to bring about change.

Just so you know, gaping holes are being punched in this erroneous assumption.

In August 2015, the scientific journal *Nature* published a socks-knocking study proving that things over here (say, our thoughts) influence things over there. It's one of quantum theory's fundamental claims: that objects separated by great distance instantaneously affect each other's behavior. The fact that two entangled electrons in diamond crystals, separated by nearly a mile, changed spins simultaneously was kinda a big blow to old-school physics.

Although these types of nonlocal experiments have been going on since the '70s (I wrote about Bell's theorem, a cornerstone of quantum mechanics, in *E-Squared*), this experiment at Delft University of Technology was emblazoned across *The New York Times* and media outlets across the world because the physicists who conducted the experiments ruled out all hidden variables and categorically proved that we are all entangled (what a physicist might say) and connected (what a guru might say). In other words, our consciousness has butt-kicking power.

Six Degrees of Kevin Bacon

*"I'm big because I'm connected to the universe,
and the universe is connected to me."*

— Neil deGrasse Tyson, astrophysicist

In the new story, the quantum story where everything is connected, we recognize that each of us is an integral part of the cosmic energy field. Where we shine our spotlight literally makes ripples. What we animate with our attention affects not just our personal experience, but the experience of the whole universe. Every act, thought, belief has cosmic significance.

According to Heisenberg (the German physicist, not the TV character in New Mexico), we affect and change everything we observe. He called it "disturbing the observed." *Disturb*, to a physicist, means to change or modify the molecules, the atoms, the energy that makes up a physical thing. Everything I observe, everything I do, affects everything else.

Princeton physics professor John Wheeler famously said, "Sorry, folks, but it's no longer valid to see ourselves as mere onlookers." He called it one of the "deep, happy mysteries" that, at all times, we interact with and influence the world we observe.

This is what we do all day, every day. We look out at the world with our biases and beliefs and opinions and "disturb" the world.

When we observe the world from a resonant field of gratitude—when we use our attention to spot beauty, to gaze at wonder—we emit a frequency of love, of magic, of miracles. This joy oscillation is the most powerful frequency on the planet and has the capability of radically uplifting the world.

All of us wildly underestimate the impact we have on each other. We discount the tremendous effect even the smallest act has on all of humanity.

Anytime I love myself more, I send love out into the bigger whole. Anytime I forgive someone who allegedly "wronged" me, I help heal the planet. The small invisible things that many don't validate or think important have great healing power. Grabbing the shopping bags of the 82-year-old widow may never go viral on Facebook, but on some level, it's going out, making waves in the invisible energy field that forms the blueprint for the material world.

Everything I do affects everything else.

Any act of love, even a small one like making goofy faces at a baby, radios a certain frequency out across the universe. Every thought, every action, emits invisible subterranean threads.

How cool is it that by believing in oneness, by choosing to add energy to the resonant field of gratitude and joy, you can fundamentally *change* the world? Getting happy, we now know, is good for the planet. You don't have to march for peace (although you may want to) or fast for three weeks. You can enlarge the conversation by taking your focus off the negative and noticing all the things that are going right, taking a stand for the goodness of humanity.

∝

All of us have two main frequencies. The first, driven by the amygdala, kicks in when we watch a disturbing news story. It sends out a frequency of *Wow! It's a dog-eat-dog world out there. I'd better protect myself. Better shut down.*

The other frequency, the one that knows reality is never frightening, radios out love and trust in our fellow humans. By believing in oneness, in joy, we can, together, literally rewrite the energy field of the planet.

A study by James Fowler of the University of California–San Diego and Nicholas Christakis of Harvard showed that just observing generosity spurs acts of good. So one person feeding a quarter into an expired parking meter can create a domino effect, inspiring dozens and even hundreds of people to be generous. Their study, funded by the National Institute on Aging, proved that just watching someone perform a good deed—say, a homeless guy returning an expensive bracelet or a waitress buying lunch for a table of servicemen—inspires people to pay it forward. They found it can go on for three degrees—in other words, your action inspires my action that inspires someone else's action.

But I say that's an underestimate. A guy in Canada's Okanagan Valley told me about the time he drove up to the window of a Tim Hortons in Winfield, British Columbia, only to be informed that his coffee had been taken care of by the person in front of him. Inspired, he decided to "pay it forward" to the next car in line.

Later, he was talking to his neighbor who works there, who told him the paying it forward went on for a full four and a half hours. *Four and a half hours* of unbridled generosity.

This is no small thing. One act of generosity—one germ of love, of hope, of optimism—can multiply and become a huge force for love.

PART II

YOUR THANK & GROW
RICH PORTFOLIO

*"When I think about creating abundance, it's
not about creating a life of luxury; it's about creating
a life of possibility. It is about taking that which
was scarce and making it abundant."*

— PETER DIAMANDIS, FOUNDER
OF THE XPRIZE FOUNDATION

4

BECOMING THE WARREN
BUFFETT OF HAPPINESS

"I want to make myself so happy
that others get happy just looking at me."

— YOGI BHAJAN, SPIRITUAL TEACHER WHO
INTRODUCED KUNDALINI YOGA TO THE U.S.

I should get this out on the table right now. This book won't do a thing for your 401(k) or help you secure the McMansion you pasted onto your vision board. It's not about getting rich in the traditional sense.

Thank & Grow Rich is about building a different kind of portfolio, a portfolio that appreciates and expands the deep and unceasing abundance you already have. Its purpose is to grow equity in the love, creativity, and beauty that's already inside you.

There's nothing wrong with financial capital, but let me be very clear. It's incapable of bringing any measure of real happiness.

We are people who need to love. To the degree that we are able to do that, we are happy and fulfilled.

When the end game is a whole stack of money in the bank, we forfeit our precious time, our values, and the day-to-day awareness of our true calling.

Our incessant search for legal tender often separates us from the important things we already have—our families, our creativity, our gorgeous, life-sustaining planet—and the important things we really want—freedom, deeper connections, meaningful work.

This book is about rediscovering your other riches, your important riches. Instead of building equity and amassing more stuff, you'll compound the Divine inheritance you were given coming in.

Real security lies not in collecting gold coins, but in knowing that anytime you move toward the thing that gives you chills, the thing that makes you feel most alive, you will be blessed . . . you will be gloriously provided for. The universe, believe it or not, will actually conspire to help you.

What could provide more security than knowing anything you could ever want is available—not through your stock portfolio, but by the universe that created you for the sole purpose of expanding its glory?

What could elicit more joy than realizing your assignment here on this big ball hurtling through space is to have fun, follow the GPS of your joy, and create the good, the holy, and the beautiful.

The Old Paradigm

> *"This idea that there is a problem . . .*
> *that's the wild hair in the ass of humanity."*

— ADYASHANTI, SPIRITUAL TEACHER

The world is a magical place. What we've been offered so far is anything but.

Let's start with our current economic system. It's made up. It's a random agreement we've all agreed to participate in. But it's not real.

It was designed by the reptilian part of our brain, the part that's scared, the part that hollers, *Danger! Watch out! Protect yourself!*

It's based on artificial lack and rampant, unsatisfying consumerism. It can never give us what we really want. One of its key tenets, in fact, is to encourage us to seek things we already have. To keep the economy growing— the holy grail, according to the current paradigm—we've been forced to monetize all the gifts we were given coming in . . . things like health, water, entertainment, food.

Even self-help books like this promote the very peace and well-being you already have—or did, before we laid our economic story on top of it.

Until our financial paradigms got all up in Mother Nature's face, we were gifted with everything we could possibly need.

When you build anything, particularly an economic system, on faulty information, it should come as no surprise when it fails to satisfy.

Here are a few of the bald-faced premises upon which the official dogma of the Western world is built:

1. That we face an indifferent universe. Every thing we do, every thing we believe, is predicated on the idea that we live in an indifferent and sometimes even antagonistic universe. To be successful, we think we must bend it to our will. Exert control, use discipline. To believe the universe might know what it's doing, to think it might actually love us and have a plan for our lives, is antithetical to every lesson economists teach.

Is it really just a chance coincidence of random molecules that we are conscious and breathing and listening to Israel Kamakawiwo'ole play "Over the Rainbow" on a ukulele?

Once you get on the joy and gratitude frequency, you come to see that the universe is not only a co-creative force, but it's your strongest ally.

2. That there's scarcity and lack. The current economic system touts insufficiency, promotes the preposterous notion that important things are missing in your life.

Once it supplied all your basic needs (food and shelter, both of which were originally provided for free by Mother Nature), it was forced to come up with fake stuff to sell you—things like deodorant, plastic banana slicers, dancing Santa decorations, and other things that don't serve human happiness. In many ways, the economy Adam Smith helped create is little more than a government-sponsored pyramid scheme.

The assumption of scarcity is one of the central axioms of economics. It's regarded as objective truth. However, like most "objective truths," it's nothing but a projection. Like the people watching shadows in Plato's cave, we must break free from our chains. Only then can we see clearly the world's wild abundance.

And I'm not talking just metaphysically. Vast quantities of food, energy, and other resources go to waste every day. Yes, half the world is starving, but the other half throws away more than enough to feed them. There *is* and always has been more than enough to go around.

Even more abundant than the material world is the spiritual world: the creations of the human mind—songs, stories, films, ideas—all the stuff we call intellectual property.

Once we take off the blinders, throw overboard the story we've been sold, we can see how truly abundant the world really is.

3. **That we're separate.** The current financial system is based on the idea that each of us is an isolated fragment, disconnected from each other and from nature. It operates under the false assumption that what happens to someone over in Africa has no bearing on you or me. It's based on the idea that we can pollute this river over there or extract that ore down there without affecting ourselves.

Any Economics 101 professor will tell you that maximizing self-interest is normal, that competition is in your DNA.

But when we give up our cultural story that it's a dog-eat-dog, every-man-for-himself world, we can't help but notice that human cooperation is actually the norm. People love to help each other. Ask for directions if you don't believe me. People will fall all over themselves to help.

I would argue that giving to your fellow man is a universal and basic human need.

Tim Cahill, founding editor of *Outside* magazine, told me this story when we were in Namibia a few years ago:

While walking to the Swakopmund Convention Center for a presentation he was giving to the Adventure Travel

Trade Association, he asked a local, balancing a basket on her head, for the quickest route.

Noticing this stranger was on foot, she asked him, "What time do you need to be there?"

When he told her, she immediately pivoted and said, "C'mon. Let's go back for my car. Otherwise, you'll never make it."

This is who we really are, lovers of life just waiting for the chance to help.

My daughter, a card-carrying member of Oxfam, helped host what the international confederation calls a Hunger Banquet at her college every year.

Upon arrival, each guest drew a random ticket assignment to a particular "seat" at the world's economic table. Fifty-six percent (representing those who live in dire poverty) sat on the floor and got maybe a handful of rice and dirty water. The 42 percent who represented the middle class might have gotten a sandwich and a card table. The remaining 2 percent got white tablecloths, china, and a feast fit for a king.

The purpose of the banquet was to open our eyes to the fact that economic disparity, income, and available resources depend a lot on randomness and dumb luck.

But what has ended up happening (and this is where our notions of the world get seriously threatened) at these Hunger Banquets that Oxfam has staged in dozens of countries is that the 2 percent, when faced head-on with the 56 percent sitting on the floor, has ended up sharing their gnocchi, asparagus, and artichokes in pesto cream sauce.

Given the chance, people consistently do the right thing. This is what our inner impulses instruct us to do. This is what's true.

Once we let go of our ridiculous notions about "the way the world works," we get ample proof that there's absolutely no need to protect ourselves from each other, from nature's cruelty, or from our own inner impulses.

4. **That our purpose in life is to value things that just don't matter.** The economic system, as it currently reigns, encourages us to go against our highest nature. It encourages us to seek money above all else. It creates a hierarchy that certain people are better than others. It tells us that having more stuff makes us happier. It teaches us to hoard resources, to value a big car more than, say, an old-growth forest. Anyone who has ever spent time in an old-growth forest can tell you there's a lot more satisfaction to be found under a 2,000-year-old redwood than in the Lincoln MKX Matthew McConaughey drives around in TV commercials.

Our overblown consumer culture is a massive exercise in missing the point.

What the current financial paradigm offers us is not natural. It's not what we really want. The best things in life, as the old saying goes, are not things. Derek Sivers— the brilliant entrepreneur who started CD Baby and sold it for $22 million, 95 percent of which he gave to charity— said he'd love to buy trained parrots to fly around every mall in America squawking, "It won't make you happy. It won't make you happy. It's not what you really want."

What we *do* really want is to give of our gifts and talents, to be of service. We want to love. We want to be generous. We *need* to do these things. It's what makes us happy, what brings us alive.

Real security lies in becoming more of who we really are, in traveling light, being free in mind. Money, which is nothing but a bunch of green paper and plastic cards and numbers in a virtual cloud somewhere, is temporary, ephemeral, malleable. It's a symbol and works best when it's circulated. It gets stagnant sitting in one man's hedge fund.

Speaking of hedge funds, I think it's important to point out that villainizing hedge-fund managers and AIG for writing $3 trillion in unregulated derivatives is not the answer. CEOs making $500 million are as much a victim of the current financial paradigm as the rest of us.

I've often argued that amassing $10 billion, the amount Donald Trump claims to be worth, is not that different from stockpiling old newspapers, leaky buckets, and all the other junk collecting in the homes of the dysfunctional folks we watch on the A&E show *Hoarders*. Having too much money throws off perspective, causing stupid moves like buying stuff you won't use or don't even really want except that our current economic system has deluded you into believing more stuff makes you happier. As Frank Lloyd Wright once pointed out, "Wealthy people are little more than janitors for their possessions."

Tom Shadyac, the famous writer/director of *Ace Ventura*, *Liar Liar*, *Bruce Almighty*, and other Hollywood hits, seconds Wright's conclusion. "Money and possessions are a trap," he says, explaining why he chose to ditch his 17,000-square-foot compound for a 100-foot double-wide. "Spending our time accruing comfort and material possessions only inhibits and complicates happiness."

Money Is Just a Story

> *"Remember . . . nobody wins unless everybody wins."*
> — BRUCE SPRINGSTEEN, ROCK STAR

Pointing fingers only exacerbates the problem. Calling out "bad guys" instead of asking "Where is that place inside me that feels I don't have enough?" only keeps us stuck in the problem. Are we really greedy? Or are we just scared?

Just so you know, most millionaires worry about money as much as—if not more than—you do. They often find it hard to trust and difficult to let go, and feel guilty because, hey, they're living the dream and why are they still dissatisfied?

Wealth is far from a synonym for *security*. It often breeds the opposite, building a wall that blocks our true wealth—our common humanity and our inclinations to create and give and spread joy.

The only thing the one-percenters have over the average Joes is this: They already know that accumulating money doesn't bring lasting happiness. They've already figured out that having a gazillion dollars in the bank doesn't produce the profound contentment after which the rest of us lust.

Take Ken Behring, for example. Growing up in Depression-era Wisconsin in a house without central heat or hot water, Behring fell for the lie that he'd be happy if only he were rich. As a young boy, he mowed lawns, caddied at golf courses, delivered newspapers.

He had spunk and drive and eventually became an über-successful real estate developer. By the time he was 27, he was a millionaire. And he got all the stuff he thought he wanted: a big house, a boat, fancy cars.

When that didn't bring any real happiness, he tried "better stuff": bigger houses, a bigger yacht, fancier cars.

Eventually, that began to reek like the other stuff. Maybe he was going for the "wrong stuff"; maybe he

33

should try "different stuff." Maybe buying the Seattle Seahawks would make him happy.

Nope, foiled again. He eventually sold his professional football team and started hunting in Africa, flying over in his private jet. When he could, he'd take supplies, books, and medicine for the local guides and their families.

LDS Philanthropies (the charitable branch of the Church of Latter-Day Saints) heard about his trips and asked if he'd be willing to make a detour, to drop off supplies to Kosovo war refugees. After loading up 15 tons of canned meat, they noticed extra room and added six wheelchairs.

While in Romania, Behring, who passed out the wheelchairs himself, was grabbed by one of the young refugees, who had stepped on a land mine and lost his legs.

"Don't leave just yet," said the grateful young boy, who refused to let go of Behring's leg. "I want to memorize your face so when we meet again in heaven, I can thank you one more time."

"It was the first time I ever felt real joy," says Behring, who has since given away nearly a million bright red wheelchairs. "It changed my life. This [charitable work] is the greatest thing I have ever achieved in my life."

The good news is that because our financial system is an antiquated cultural story, it can be changed.

It starts with a new definition of *wealth*: the ease and freedom to be generous. The ease and freedom to pursue your dreams. The ease and freedom to live for the upliftment of all creation.

Choosing the joy and gratitude frequency generates a different kind of capital, one that feeds the soul, one that serves your real desires—to be of service, to be a channel for love, to create insanely beautiful things.

5

FINANCIAL WEALTH IS A SIDE EFFECT OF YOUR REAL RICHES

"What we need is people who specialize in the impossible."
— THEODORE ROETHKE,
PULITZER PRIZE—WINNING POET

SantaCon, a giant pub crawl for people dressed in Santa costumes, is held annually in 51 countries. In Lawrence, where I live, it raises money for the humane society, so quite naturally, there are Santa rules. Things like "Don't be *that* Santa," "Don't f**k with kids," and "Don't get arrested." But my favorite rule is "A Santa hat is not enough." In other words, you gotta go all in, top to bottom.

It's also a useful guideline for making the most of the Thank & Grow Rich investment portfolio I'm about to introduce.

As I said, you already have every one of these assets. But until you dive in, top to bottom, you may not be aware of their massive returns and life-changing performance.

How to dive in:

1. **Start identifying good things in your life.** Make this an active practice. Do it as if your life depended on it. Gratitude, as I've already mentioned, creates cataclysmic reverberations. It literally changes things. I call this *alchemic capital.*

2. **Turn your life over to the big mystery.** This promotes *spiritual capital.* We'll talk more about each of these investments here in a minute.

3. **Move toward that which makes you feel most alive.** In Japan, they call it *waku waku.* You can actually feel it in your body. It's your most reliable GPS for discovering your already-installed *creative capital.* And just so you know, it's not reserved for artists.

4. **Relax and have more fun.** Each of us only gets so many heartbeats. Since we never know exactly how many, every day should be used to generate *adventure capital.*

5. **Share your good luck.** Spread it around. Save a life. Serve the planet. This investment creates *social capital.* We're connected to everyone anyway. Might as well be friends.

Alchemic Capital

> *"The man who views himself the same at 50*
> *as he did at 20 has wasted 30 years of his life."*
>
> — MUHAMMAD ALI, PRIZEFIGHTER

This is an important vehicle of capital that you've likely run from most of your life. It's the capital of change, of evolution. Specifically, it's where you tap into your own inner magic, using it to effect change. In yourself. In the collective conscious. In the universe.

Alchemy, the medieval forerunner of chemistry, was the practice of transforming matter. It largely disappeared after the advent of the periodic table, but modern-day physicists tell us we practice alchemy (well, they don't use that exact word) every time we observe anything. When we "pay attention" to something (be it the annoying gum chewing of the taxi driver or the smile of our beloved), we "buy" that experience. We feed it with our attention. We literally make it grow. What we focus on expands. We change things all the time . . . except when we continue to expect and focus on the exact same things we expected and focused on yesterday.

Many of us resist change, fear it, exert contortive efforts to avoid it. But change is inevitable and is meant to work for the greater good of all.

Would you really want to be in the same place (the same head space, the same habits, the same cramped worldview) ten years from now?

Not me. I hope my life is completely unrecognizable in ten years. Because that means I allowed the universe, which is so much wiser and more beautiful than I can even conceive, have its way with me. Sure, I could clutch at my life, unwisely hold tight to what's here now. But when I come from that restricted space, I'm always miserable.

Spiritual Capital

> *"God comes to you disguised as your life."*
>
> — PAULA D'ARCY, WRITER AND RETREAT LEADER

We're all born with huge reserves of spiritual capital. Very few of us maximize its potential or allow it to appreciate. Nowhere is the return greater.

So why have we relegated our spiritual capital to the back of the dusty vault, hardly even registering its existence? Here are the top three reasons.

1. **Somewhere along the way, spirituality took an uncool turn.** It got co-opted by a bunch of fundamentalist religions who turned God into a judgmental prick. They introduced us to a God of "dont's" and gave us a list of rules and commandments that rein in our natural impulses.

2. **The perks got pushed into the future.** Self-appointed spiritual purveyors also forget to mention that God (or the FP or the Divine Energy) is available to enjoy and use now. Asking us to wait for the bennies is to miss the whole point.

3. **It's, well, invisible.** It sounds insane. Trusting in an invisible force. Turning your life over to something that's nothing to the eyeballs.

My current favorite definition of *spirituality* comes from Rainn Wilson, the actor who played nerdy paper salesman Dwight Schrute on NBC's *The Office*. His website SoulPancake (Spirit Taco was taken) was created to, as he says, "chew on life's big questions."

Here's how he described it on a recent podcast:

> We humans have a whole bunch of things in common with monkeys. We both enjoy bananas, groom each other, spend a lot of time on our hair. We both have a pecking order, form tribes, and sometimes when we're really mad, we throw feces.
>
> There's nothing wrong with these things per se. But spirituality is everything we don't have in common with monkeys. It's that part of us that creates beautiful works of art, that has inspiring conversations, that contemplates meaning, that strives to be in service to other people.

So how do you connect with this non-monkey part of yourself? You follow your joy. You move toward your impulse of bliss. If you follow that path, invest your energy in the invisible force that powers the universe, there is never any doubt about what to do next or which path to follow.

Because we're taught just the opposite (get good grades, make sure people like you, stop running around and whooping like a wild banshee), we spend our lives wondering, *What does God want from me? What am I supposed to do with my life?* It's all there in living color.

Spiritual capital is getting in touch with what I call the field of infinite potentiality. Others call it God. Or Buddha. Or Divine Intelligence. It matters not one whit what you call it. What matters is that you call it forth. That you recognize its immense power and real-time practicality.

Creative Capital

*"Joy is in everything and anything we might experience.
We just have to have the courage to turn against our
habitual lifestyle and engage in unconventional living."*

— JON KRAKAUER, WRITER AND MOUNTAINEER

Like spiritual capital, this exciting investment opportunity has no floor, no ceiling. And we are all blessed with an infinite supply. We all have the ability to build empires out of our imaginations. The muses have an unlimited supply of songs, films, books, inventions, ideas, and lots of other brilliant things that I can't list because they haven't been birthed yet. They're currently "advertising" for humans to pilot them into existence.

The universe needs you to help it expand. We're all asked to bring new things to light. It's holy work, and we're all called.

To access your creative capital, you just have to follow your beeps. You have to use your internal GPS, the Divine Buzz. It's the thing you'd want to do if you'd never heard the word *money*. You'll recognize it when you feel the chills, when you notice the excitement and joy in your body.

Follow what most excites you and the right people, the right materials, the right opportunities will show up.

Dances with Wolves, *Black or White*, and *Bull Durham* are just a few films I've loved because a human named Kevin Costner followed his beeps.

One day when he was a senior at Cal State–Fullerton, he was sitting in an accounting class, flipping through the college newspaper. Until that point, his academic career had been rather, well, lackluster. He recognized he wasn't that motivated and, in fact, had no idea what he wanted to do with the business degree he was pursuing, mostly because, well, what else was he going to do after graduating from high school?

He happened to notice an ad in the back of the college newspaper. The drama department was auditioning for the play *Rumpelstiltskin*. Kevin had never acted (he was a baseball player and sang in the church choir), but to his surprise the hair on the back of his neck stood up. He knew, with a passion he'd never felt before, that he was going to be at that audition.

"I closed the paper and sat there listening to the teacher drone on and on, but I was excited in a way I hadn't been since I started college. I was excited the way a kid is excited," he said.

On the way to the audition, the accelerator pedal on his pickup got stuck, causing it to barrel down the highway at 80 mph. He felt sure he was going to crash into something and die, kill someone, or maybe both. Luckily, he found the presence of mind to throw the clutch into neutral, turn off the ignition, and let it roll, screeching all the way to the side of the road.

Kevin jumped out of the car, leaped over the fence, and ran the rest of the way to the audition.

I'd love to tell you his valiant bravery won him the part. But I can't. As he says, "I didn't have any skill. I wasn't any good."

But his imagination began to burn with possibilities. He became jump-up-and-down excited. He had found his creative capital.

"I didn't care to improve in accounting," he says, "but when I found acting I knew it was something I could care about. Something I wanted to learn."

He became the student he never was in college. He framed houses during the day and then hustled to acting class one, two, three nights a week.

"I fell in love with something. I didn't know if I could make a living at it, but I didn't care. I finally shook loose from the uncertainty of what I was going to do with my life."

Adventure Capital

"Let's take to the streets with our messy, imperfect, wild, stretch-marked, wonderful, heartbreaking, grace-filled, and joyful lives."

— BRENÉ BROWN,
AUTHOR OF *THE GIFTS OF IMPERFECTION*

Also known as *experiential capital* or *have-a-whooping-good-time capital*, this invaluable investment turns every day into an adventure.

It's important to note that adventures don't just happen on treks in the Himalayas or at Burning Man. They happen anytime you consciously choose to step into an unfamiliar place. To shake things up a bit. It can be something simple like taking a different route to work, trying a new dish on the menu, or simply saying "yes" to something to which you normally say "no."

When you step out of your box of familiarity, your senses become heightened. Life takes on a new shade; it seems sweeter, more alive.

I call it being a joy ambassador. My friends and I consciously spread molecules of joy and happiness wherever we go. It's not uncommon to get comments like, "You guys are just too happy. What are you on?"

Having public adventures might seem like a small thing. But I consider it an important public service. In our cosmically connected world, every act is a service. At all times, we're contributing to the collective consciousness.

Social Capital

"Spend your life doing strange things with weird people."

— JEROME JARRE,
20-SOMETHING SOCIAL MEDIA STAR

Remember summer camp? It didn't matter that you slept on a lumpy mattress or that the food on your plastic tray jiggled—you were wholly happy as you cooked up crazy shenanigans with your peers. You were fearless, darting through bushes without worrying about ticks or slugs or sharp metal objects.

Time was unlimited, and cheers went up whether you were throwing water balloons or spiking your bunkmate's hair with shaving cream.

So what if you weren't solving world hunger. You were fully engaged, committed, all in. Your friends, your soul mates, were right by your side scheming and dreaming.

This is blue-chip capital, my friends, worth far more than any stock portfolio.

It's a cliché that we need friends, of course, but this all-important capital should be different than having someone to whine to. It's having comrades to have fun with, to enjoy beautiful food with, to have fulfilling, meaningful conversations with. Because if you're not having fun in this lifetime, what's the point? Why bother?

Social capital means having a team to cheer you on and, when asked, to participate in your crazy schemes.

You do have crazy schemes, right? Schemes to save the world, to uplift the planet.

All of us need something important to do—a project, a mission—something that captures our imagination. Otherwise, we're like the bored family pet who jumps on guests and chews up house slippers. Only our version is buying stuff we don't need, adding nasty comments to blog posts, and obsessing over whether or not our hair is too greasy.

When you employ your natural social capital, your mission becomes living for the upliftment of all creation . . . to be a vessel for love.

PART III

GAME ON

*"What I now know is that goofing off
is actually critical to my journey in this life."*

— CHERYL RICHARDSON,
AUTHOR OF *THE ART OF EXTREME SELF-CARE*

6

Pass Go and Collect Your Gifts: A Word (or Rather, a Chapter) from Our Sponsor

"Does anyone have the foggiest idea what sort of power we so blithely invoke? We should all be wearing crash helmets . . . life preservers and signal flares."

— ANNIE DILLARD,
AUTHOR OF *PILGRIM AT TINKER CREEK*

I'm not completely sure how this happened, but I have inadvertently become a PR person for the universe. The perks, as you can imagine, are many, but the best thing about this job is my "employer"—if you want to call this universal love energy my "boss"—doesn't ask me to pimp some useless product or lower my standards or pretend to believe in something I don't see proof of every single day.

The universe is not trying to sell anything. All it wants to do is give. And give. And give some more.

My job as one of its many "press agents" is to let you know that you are *loved* unconditionally—always, without exception, no matter what.

I'm in charge, if you will, of publicizing the fact that the universe is trying like bloody hell to interact with you. The universe (or God or the field of infinite potentiality or whatever name you want to call this energy force) wants nothing more than to bless you, to guide you, to help you create the most exciting version of yourself.

And here's the cool part. Not one thing is required of you for this to happen. You don't have to earn its favor. Or send in a coupon. You just have to release the "reality" you've been reading about in the news. You just have to make space in your consciousness for the universe to get in. You have to quit fighting life and let it be.

Not only is the old reality as passé as the bump (it's a dance, for those of you who missed the disco days), it's defective and causing you to miss the most freakin' amazing things.

You don't have to take my word for it. During the next 30 days, you will be presented with four mind-blowing blessings that will prove just how much you've missed by holding on so tight to your "fake reality."

We Give the Material World Way More Weight Than It Deserves

*"We're not just responsible for
what we do, but also for what we see."*

— MICHAEL HERR, AUTHOR OF *DISPATCHES*

It's a pretty sweet gig, speaking on behalf of the universe. And you'd think I'd have no trouble "selling" this completely awesome news.

Except there's this one tiny glitch.

Most of us here on planet Earth put all our stock in what we experience with our five senses. We continue to do this even though science has proven again and again that our senses have major design flaws.

We believe the aforementioned voices in our heads.

Instead of looking deeper, instead of relying on something that actually works, we buy into the ticker tape of nonsense that runs through our brains. We call the crazy voices reality.

But the reality we've been experiencing for the past 6,000 years is nothing but a figment of our imaginations and can be changed at any time.

I'd like to repeat that last statement. The material reality in which you have invested so heavily can be changed at any time.

Once you begin vibrating at a different frequency, the frequency of joy and gratitude, everything in your life will change. Things you never thought possible will show up. You'll probably even send me an e-mail that starts with something like, "You are never going to believe this."

Which is why I've been commissioned to offer readers four free gifts.

Each of these gifts from the universe will be custom-made just for you. So I can't promise exactly how yours will show up. But I can guarantee this: If you get on the frequency of gratitude explained in this book, you will receive the following four blessings.

1. A Personal Symbol, a Totem, a Sign That the Universe Has Your Back

You will notice this symbol showing up anytime you need reassurance or guidance. It's a hint, a wink, a nod, assuring you that you're on the right track.

I jokingly named this the Carol Burnett principle. Every night during her Emmy-winning variety show, the popular comedian would at some point pull on her earlobe. It was a sign, a way of saying hello to her grandmother who raised her.

The universe, for those of us paying attention, is every bit as generous. It constantly sends us signs, constantly lets us know, *Hey, it's going to be okay. You're all right.*

Pope Francis says that whenever he's troubled or needing comfort, he sees a white rose. That's his personal sign, directly from the Big Guy. My friend Annola is sent a crane—the bird, not the construction rig.

Blessings and signs such as these never end. Unfortunately, most of us aren't paying attention, stuck as we are in our old-school vibration. We're too busy listening to the voices and following the scripts and constructs we erroneously created to serve as our reality. On this new frequency, the channel of joy and gratitude, we begin to notice a never-ending stream of magnanimity.

2. A Magical Blessing from the Natural World

It might be from a bird or a tree or the misty river of the Milky Way flowing across the sky. When you become receptive to the beauty, the joy, and the excitement of the natural world, you're suddenly free from the boundaries of human existence.

Rachel Carson called it "a sense of wonder" and said "it provides an unfailing antidote against the boredom and . . . the sterile preoccupation with things that are artificial, the alienation from the sources of our strength."

Gratefully, I can report to Ms. Carson that the natural world she so loved is stepping up its game, working overtime to get our attention. And unlike Aladdin's genie, who only gave three wishes, nature keeps blessing us, day after day.

After a tour in Vietnam ended abruptly for former Marine Scott Harrison (his knee was shredded by a grenade after only seven months), he was airlifted out of the battlefield and returned to an America that, as he says, "wouldn't look a soldier in the eye."

To cope, he drank, took drugs, and "isolated," eventually migrating to San Jose, California, where he worked in a boatyard.

In his continuing effort to avoid human contact, he built a 32-foot schooner on which he sailed alone, deep into the Pacific. He was out of his mind, sobbing with grief and remorse, hoping for a big storm to capsize his boat and put him out of his misery.

Instead, on the eighth day at sea, a 30-foot whale surfaced next to his boat and looked him straight in the eye. The whale swam beside him for three or four hours.

For reasons Harrison says he can't explain, "It made me feel loved in a way I'd never been loved before."

3. A Message from the "Other Side"

. . . or what we erroneously call the other side. There really is no "other side." There's just the side we allow into our belief system. And the side we decided is mysterious and/or miraculous. The side we tuned out when dialed into the "life blows" frequency.

Some might label their "delivery man" an angel. Others might get a shout-out from a deceased relative. Or hear from a disembodied entity who's reveling in the quantum playground without the limitations of acid reflux, weight gain, and other bodily ailments.

Either way, you'll be shown that there's an incredible amount of support in many different dimensions that you have blocked out with your belief that the material world is all there is.

Because of our stubborn conviction that we need a body to communicate, we miss a lot of cool messages from our discarnate comrades. Let's just say they have a much bigger perspective. They've escaped the echo chamber of fear that we so often experience on the material plane.

When my friend Annola's dad wants to come through, he turns off the TV belonging to her daughter, his granddaughter, who was born the same week he passed. I suppose that could be annoying if you're right in the middle of an episode of *Castle*. But you gotta admit—it's hard to ignore him that way.

My friend Cindy's brother, who died in his 20s, delivers regular guidance that, as often happens when you're not viewing life from the myopic viewpoint of a body, is much clearer and more loving than the guidance she might get from a bodily bound friend.

In the beginning, she said, her intense grief thwarted his efforts to communicate . . . even though they'd made a pact in childhood that whoever went first would come back to say hi.

She said to him one day, "Ya know, it would be a lot easier if you could figure out a clear way to make your presence known—like, how about using electronics?"

A couple of days later, she was downstairs folding laundry when she heard booming music upstairs. She was irritated, wondering what in the heck her husband was doing. She met him in the hallway, where he, too, was heading toward the extremely *loud* music coming from the bathroom. An ear-piercing rendition of one of her brother's favorite songs was playing on a radio they'd left in the bathroom as a decoration.

The weirdest part is that radio—which they hadn't used in years—had no batteries.

4. A Clear Sign That Something You've Long Clung to as Absolute Fact Is Not True at All

Take money, for example. A very popular "absolute fact" is that money is limited and hard to come by. Twenty years ago, when I decided to enroll in a $1,500 workshop in Cape Cod, I was dabbling in freelance writing. Most people would call it being unemployed. I had maybe $59 in my checking account.

I resolved to go to the workshop, even though the responses from the three friends I was silly enough to mention it to went something like this:

- "Dream on!"
- "Fat chance."
- "When pigs fly."

But I happen to know the universe can be a crafty mother, so I sent in my $50 deposit. When you have $59 left in your checking account, it's very easy to let go of all notions you are capable of handling money on your own. I had no choice but to let go of the "absolute fact" I could not afford the workshop.

The very night I sent in my deposit, a woman I barely knew called me to do a project for her new company. She requested an article in *Self* magazine about the cloth prosthetics she invented for breast-cancer patients.

The project took me all of two hours; the exposure earned her nearly a quarter million dollars and made me wonder, *Why didn't I charge a percentage instead of a flat fee?* But the $2,000 she paid me was the exact amount I needed for the workshop and the airfare to get there.

I'm happy to report that I refrained from calling my friends and saying "Take that, suckers." Even if I did probably sorta casually paraphrase the quote attributed to Goethe about boldness having "genius, power, and magic."

Another example that life is not cut-and-dried comes from Deepak Chopra. Or rather, his assistant, who was trying desperately to reach him. Unfortunately, he was in Africa, in a region far from phones, Internet, and all the other devices we depend on for communication with others. At that point, most people would accept the "absolute fact" that he was off the grid and unreachable. Instead, she employed what I call the 101 Dalmatians Principle, which posits that we are interconnected with everyone and everything through an invisible field of intelligence and energy.

She began sending out this message: "Deepak, I really need you to call me. Deepak, call me now."

I'm sure you can guess the end of the story. Within a few hours, Deepak called.

Who Do I Think I Am—Santa Claus?

"The miracle of gratitude is that it shifts your perception to such an extent that it changes the world you see."

— ROBERT HOLDEN, HAPPINESS EXPERT

You're probably wondering how I can be so bold as to promise all these perks from the universe. How can I be so sure these gifts will actually show?

The reason I can so confidently and blithely make these promises is because every one of these gifts and blessings is already available, already lined up outside your door. These love notes from the universe are waiting for you to notice, waiting for you to tune in.

So, no, you probably don't have Kim Kardashian's butt. Or LeBron James's MVP trophies. But you do have lots of other stuff. Methinks it's time to lighten up. Have some fun. Quit wanting what you don't have. And start loving all that you do.

Your Initial Thank & Grow Rich Earnings Report

> *"Cover all five bases, and you'll have
> a portfolio that can win in any market."*
> — JIM CRAMER, HOST OF *MAD MONEY*

As any portfolio manager will tell you, diversifying your investments is the best long-term strategy. Let's start with a snapshot of where you are today. That way we can track the performance and ROI (return on investment) of your assets during the next 30 days.

Using the definition for each of the investment vehicles we discussed in Chapter 5, please rank by circling your current equity on a scale of 1 to 10. For example, if you feel your creative currency is revved up and producing masterpieces, circle 10. If your spiritual currency, on the other hand, needs work, you might want to give it a 2 or a 3.

Ready?

TODAY'S DATE: _____

LOVE

80.9 + 5.6 (6.92%)

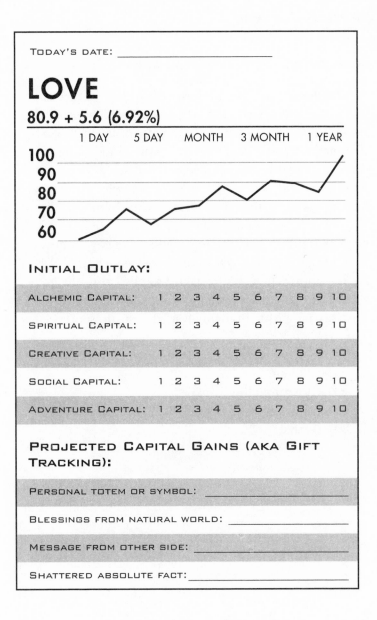

	1 DAY	5 DAY	MONTH	3 MONTH	1 YEAR

INITIAL OUTLAY:

ALCHEMIC CAPITAL: 1 2 3 4 5 6 7 8 9 10

SPIRITUAL CAPITAL: 1 2 3 4 5 6 7 8 9 10

CREATIVE CAPITAL: 1 2 3 4 5 6 7 8 9 10

SOCIAL CAPITAL: 1 2 3 4 5 6 7 8 9 10

ADVENTURE CAPITAL: 1 2 3 4 5 6 7 8 9 10

PROJECTED CAPITAL GAINS (AKA GIFT TRACKING):

PERSONAL TOTEM OR SYMBOL: _____

BLESSINGS FROM NATURAL WORLD: _____

MESSAGE FROM OTHER SIDE: _____

SHATTERED ABSOLUTE FACT: _____

Share Your Gifts with Others—Literally

In addition to your personal earnings report, I hope you'll boogie on over to the Thank & Grow Rich Instagram community. I hope you'll share your gifts (literally) by snapping photos of, say, your totem or your blessing from the natural world. I've discovered that we gain strength by sharing with what I like to call possibility posses (née power posses). As they used to say on the Muppets, "Even weirdos can be a family." Of course, we're only weirdos because we defy society's prescription. We pay witness to the fact that when we get on the right frequency, miracles are the norm. The news media offers one story, one probability. But, as we are here to prove, there are a gazillion others. True spirituality will always be a team sport.

https://www.instagram.com/thankandgrowrich
#T&GRtotem
#T&GRnaturalbling
#T&GRmessage
#T&GRshatteredfact

7

THE ONLY PARTY
GAME YOU REALLY NEED

"Overthrow the sour, puckered hallucination
that is mistakenly referred to as reality."

— ROB BREZSNY, ASTROLOGER

Tesla Motors recently rolled out an autopilot feature in its S and X series cars. Using 12 ultrasonic sensors, a front-windshield camera, and long-distance radar, this newfangled technology allows drivers to basically sit back and let the car do the heavy lifting. My friend Cindy, after test-driving one in Kansas City, reported that, like life, it's über-challenging to take your hands off the steering wheel.

While driving sans hands has its bennies, it also sets off a red-alert alarm in your brain.

We're taught, after all, that our job is to keep our eyes peering nervously out the windshield. That it's up to us to figure life out, that we're required to be vigilantly on the lookout for danger ahead.

Most of us believe that not only do we need to keep our eye on the ball of potential problems, but that once we spot them, we must think our way out. We believe if we just exert enough mental effort, we will pull up a solution to whatever ails us.

But what if life actually works better when we quit gripping the steering wheel so tightly? What if those problems we're so busy solving don't actually exist?

Quit Thinking; Start Thanking

"I think and think and think, I've thought myself out
of happiness one million times, but never once into it."

— JONATHAN SAFRAN FOER,
AUTHOR OF *EVERYTHING IS ILLUMINATED*

In my quest to "heal myself," I have been to therapy, analyzed my dreams, gotten rebirthed, written scathing letters to my parents, walked on coals, and read hundreds of self-help books. Maybe thousands.

You'd think I'd be hanging out with Oprah by now. But it wasn't until I embarked on a simple practice of gratitude that I finally got what I'd been looking for all these years.

The reason I looked down my nose at this practice that, in one way or another, has been around for thousands of years (even the Bible says, "In all things, give thanks") is because, well, it seemed way too simplistic. Getting "happy" can't be that easy. Right?

I'd been taught that the only way to "heal myself" was to put in my time, dig up my broken places. I'd been taught that if I gave enough effort, I would eventually someday "get it." Whatever "it" was.

I tried to think my way out of problems. I tried to analyze what was going wrong.

Little did I realize that all my thinking was a trap, a prison that put me over and over again in solitary confinement.

It wasn't until I began to actively look around at all my blessings that it dawned on me: *Everything is exactly perfect just the way it is. I'm exactly perfect just the way I am.*

I call it being on the frequency of joy and gratitude, turning in to the Divine Buzz (D-Buzz.) The Divine Buzz, while known by many other names, is an energetic *cha-cha-cha* of a force that wants to interact and have fun with you.

If this all sounds vague, hold on. There's a very concrete practice for connecting to the Divine Buzz. I call it AA 2.0. Unlike the first AA (Alcoholics Anonymous) with its 12 steps and nightly meetings, this process has two simple steps. At most, it takes five minutes in the morning.

It's so simple that, if I know you, you will be tempted to discount it. To write it off as beneath your time. Please do not do that.

D-Buzz is actually your natural state. As I said, it's the frequency where miracles happen.

Well-known spiritual teacher Byron Katie teaches a method of self-inquiry she calls the "The Work."

My method? Let's just call it "The Play."

Party Game #1

AA 2.0

"Joy is the most infallible sign of the existence of God."
— Longtime note on Stephen Colbert's computer

When I began focusing on what could go right (instead of the more popular viewpoint touted on CNN), I found that my so-called problems had a way of fixing themselves. I discovered the less I did, the better my life worked.

The more I identified with the invisible realm of goodness, joy, and beauty, the happier I became. The less I planned, the more magic became available.

Planning, by its very nature, is based on what we know. We can't plan for *firturjelsk*, for example. Or ask for *wemerk*. Why?

Because our limited pea brains have never heard of them.

The invisible realm has a much bigger vantage point, so when we start focusing on all that's good, the flow opens up, and experiences way better than we can imagine mysteriously line up for our enjoyment.

I started this super-easy gratitude regime right before *E-Squared* came out. I mentioned it on one of my early radio interviews. Sorta tongue in cheek, I called it AA 2.0, a take-off on the original 12-step program of Alcoholics Anonymous (AA).

Almost inadvertently, it became my mantra, my signature. Fans, who claim to have changed the word *gratitude* to *groutitude*, started sending me plaques and prisms and memes with the catchphrase from step 1.

It's the catalyst for this book and the only thing you're asked to do during this 30-day experiment.

Here's the blog post I wrote after the interview:

My name is Pam G., and I am a joy and happiness freak. To celebrate, I launched a brand-new chapter of AA.

Unlike Version 1.0, my AA stands for "Amazing Awesomeness," and it only has two steps.

- **STEP #1: Admit that . . . "something amazingly awesome is going to happen" to you today.** First thing every morning, before you throw off your covers, before you leap out of bed, before you fire up the old Mr. Coffee, proclaim to the world that something unexpected, exciting, and *amazingly awesome* is headed your way today.

  It takes, what, three, four seconds? Yet it's one of the most important things you can do each morning. The first few minutes of every day pre-paves the next 24 hours with positive expectations. It sets up a powerful intention, a forecast on which you now choose to focus.

  And it never fails to come true.

- **STEP #2: Come to believe . . . in blessings and miracles.** Pretend to be a private investigator assigned the task of finding all the beauty and largesse in the world. The dominant paradigm might suggest otherwise, but practiced with regularity, this ritual will allow you to see things in a whole different light. Instead of looking for problems, be on the hunt for blessings. You'll find, to paraphrase the description of the old radio character Chickenman, "They're everywhere. They're everywhere."

To make sure your thoughts don't return to their slacking tendencies, text (or tweet or post them on Facebook or Instagram) three blessings (aka amazing awesomeness) each morning. The only stipulation is the items on your list must be different every day.

I often liken myself to Lewis or Clark, scouting important new territory.

Because we get out of life whatever we focus upon, practicing these two simple steps has radically changed my life. It will change yours, too.

Try it for the next 30 days. Feel free to switch it up a bit, if you desire. For example, you could say, "Something magical is going to happen to me today."

But each morning, no matter how you feel, no matter what is happening, say your phrase (if you want, add a fist pump) and text three blessings (new ones, no repeats) to a group of friends. Text it to your mother, if you have to. Or write it down. Just don't repeat.

A Quick Demo

> *"Accept each minute as an unrepeatable miracle."*
>
> — STORM JAMESON, JOURNALIST

I'm a travel writer (writing about travel is one of the amazingly awesome things I get to do), so to demonstrate, here are the texts I sent during a recent adventure to Belize:

- *Thursday:* Easy, on-time flights; staying on a 7,200-acre rain-forest preserve; and drinking Argentinean wine with the resort's South African manager.

- *Friday:* Exploring a 3,000-year-old Mayan site; howler monkeys who sound like *Jurassic Park*; and rescuing my favorite hat before it plunged down an 800-foot waterfall.

- *Saturday:* Swimming three feet away from a three-foot loggerhead turtle; seeing lemon sharks, barracuda, and a giant school of blue tang; and being invited to watch the Caribbean Cup soccer finals on an outdoor TV while eating just-caught barbecued lobster.

- *Sunday:* Egrets and pelicans on my morning beach walk; mimosas and gelato before my 10 A.M. flight; and getting home 30 minutes early.

8

THE TRUTH AND MERRIMENT LEAGUE GAME AND TOY BOX

"You should be dancing in your shoes at all times."

— *THE WAY OF MASTERY*

After turning in book manuscripts, we writers always pray our editors call us immediately, gushing about how much they adore our brilliant outpouring. The sooner, the better, as far as we're concerned. Because until that moment, we tend to use our creative imaginations composing wild and crazy tales about how they're slumping over their desks gagging into their trash cans. We scroll through want ads, looking for gainful employment now that the secret's out about our glaring lack of talent.

This book was no different. Three lifetimes later, when my editor finally got back with me, she had but one main concern.

The book needs more actionable steps. She wanted exercises that readers could use to put the extreme sport of gratitude into action. Steps (7 steps to happiness, 8 steps to wealth, 18 steps to learning the watusi) and publishers of self-help books, I've learned, go together like hipsters and weird sunglasses.

I was hesitant at first. My position has always been there's only one step. No matter what you're hoping to master, no matter what you're trying to learn.

1. Get on the frequency of gratitude, of openness, of spaciousness.

2. Follow what shows up.

Enough Said—or So I Thought

"There is bad and there is good . . . And then there is crazy good."
— STEVE CHANDLER,
AUTHOR OF DOZENS OF SELF-HELP BOOKS

So about the time my editor sends her note on the manuscript, I start getting e-mails from readers.

"I like what you're saying," they wrote, "but how do I get there? How do I get on that frequency? Tell me, *puh-lease.*"

So I get it. More detail is necessary.

But I just can't bring myself to offer exercises. Or steps. Just sounds like too much work.

I've always felt my gift is sharing stories that inspire and encourage people to open to a bigger reality. The last thing I feel qualified for is telling people how to do anything. As Cheryl Strayed said in her book *Brave Enough*, "I'm not trying to be the boss of you. I'm attempting to be a better boss of me." At best, my work is aspirational. So in lieu of exercises (does anybody really do the exercises in self-help books?), I'm offering *party games*. I've already introduced the first one. Each game comes with a *party favor* (one of those stories I like to share) and *pudding* (as in "the proof is in the . . .") about a real person who tuned in to the Divine Frequency and received some kind of remarkable gift. As I always like to say, if one of us can do it, all of us can do it.

Play these games at your own speed. In your own way. That might mean ignoring them completely. The only requirement for tuning in to the joy and gratitude frequency, for building your Thank & Grow Rich portfolio, is the five-minute AA 2.0 in the morning.

9

~

"You're a Pirate.
I'm a Space Alien. Go."
26 More Party Games

"Carpe the f%k out of this diem."*

— Line on my favorite pair of winter socks

Feel free to approach this section on a need-to-use basis. Or, if you're like me, and delight in having lots of party games in your game closet, why not join the Thank & Grow Rich scavenger hunt? Each of the following games comes with a suggested S&F (that's "selfie and friends") that we'd all love to see and applaud on Instagram and/or Facebook.

The only rule? Make it F.U.N.

~

Amassing Alchemic Capital

"The bliss, the wisdom, the creativity, the laughter,
the friendships, the joy, the serenity and the peace that
have been, for the most part,
seen as an impossible dream will become
your most ordinary state of being."

— THE WAY OF MASTERY

More than another book on counting blessings, this is a book about climate change. Changing the climate of your energy field, upgrading the resonance with which you perceive the world.

Practicing gratitude, more than penciling a written list, is to practice alchemy. Looking for the good in life literally changes things. Physically changes things. Financially changes things. Mentally and emotionally changes things. It literally rearranges atoms and reconfigures molecules.

Cynics like to discount gratitude, downgrade it as sweet, nice, something for naïve Pollyannas.

What I've discovered is that living on the frequency of joy and gratitude causes cataclysmic reverberations.

PARTY GAME #2

Make a List of All the Ridiculously Beautiful Things You Already Have

"I can understand wanting a million dollars, but once you get much beyond that, I have to tell you—it's the same hamburger."
— BILL GATES,
BUSINESS MAGNATE WHO CO-FOUNDED MICROSOFT

When you're on the frequency of gratitude, you know you have everything. You know nothing is missing. You know nothing could ever *be* missing.

To make lists of what you want is to separate yourself from the very things on your list.

Gratitude says, "I already have these things (how else would I have noticed them?), and I'm going to say thanks and sing and dance and carry on in sheer joy."

So in this game, instead of making lists (and vision boards) of things you'd like to receive, compose a list of all the things you already have. Things you're grateful for *now*.

If you're not playing with and appreciating "the toys" you have now, why expect new ones? Why even *want* new ones?

So, yeah, vision boards are great. But today, make lists of all the ridiculously beautiful things you already have.

#S&F
Show us one of your "treasured things."

The Party Favor: Let Magic Unfold

*"Find the glory inside yourself . . . so you can dance . . . with a
little more . . . abandon, with a little more shaking–those–hips."*

— BILLY FINGERS, BROTHER OF AUTHOR ANNIE KAGAN

Here's the thing.

If you attempt to make lasagna with a cake mix, you're
never going to end up with the layered Italian dish that's
widely credited as being the world's first pasta recipe.

If you use a map of Peoria to navigate Los Angeles,
you'll probably never find Rodeo Drive, Hollywood Boule-
vard, or Venice Beach.

Likewise, if you want to live a happy and meaningful life, it's imperative to recognize you've been using the
wrong tools.

For a very long time.

The only way to achieve peace of mind and the joy
that is your birthright is to ditch the old cake mix, to
throw overboard the old map.

We've spent the last 6,000 years using our consciousness to create what any halfway intelligent person can tell
you is a big hot mess. In our consciousness (which is the
Play-Doh of the universe), we've manufactured a complex
maze of beliefs and expectations, most of which have no
bearing on reality at all. Sadly, we've gotten horribly lost
within that labyrinth of beliefs.

We've forgotten that we're here to expand God, to
experience joy, to love the holy sh#t out of everything.
Instead of laughing and playing and delighting in the
Play-Doh, we started taking our lives way too seriously.

It is only our oh-so-intense seriousness that is holding the world in place. We have become so determined to
fix our problems, to follow the seven steps to success, that

we have completely forfeited the joy and the glee and the creative play.

If we really want to find peace and meaning, we must admit that life itself doesn't suck, just the tools we've been using to navigate it.

The tools we humans currently use to concoct our viewpoint of the world are the intellect and the five senses, which anybody who studies these things can tell you do not show us reality. In any sense of the word.

Depending on the intellect to solve problems or the five senses for a reality fix is like using that map of Peoria. Both of them show us a hologram that is no more real than R2-D2's projection of Princess Leia. The insanity of our times is we've become identified with the erroneous hologram. We actually believe this condensed version of ourselves is who we are.

We actually bought this big joke that we could be separate from our Source . . . that we could disconnect from the energy field. When in truth we are connected and in perfect communion with the whole of creation.

We are part of the FP—the energy field some people call *God* or *the universe*. The synonym you use doesn't matter. What *does* matter is being aware of it and knowing that everything is but a temporary modification of this one fundamental energy.

The only tool that will ever get us out of the elaborate maze we temporarily created is reliance on the invisible connection that drives the universe. That's it. The rest is but a ruse.

If you are unhappy, why would you turn to the limited hologram that your limited intellect (no offense) and your limited five senses have composed so far? To quote Dr. Phil, "How's that working for you?"

The Pudding

> *"Scientists are slowly waking up to an inconvenient*
> *truth—the universe looks suspiciously like a fix."*
>
> — PAUL DAVIES,
> PHYSICIST, COSMOLOGIST, AND ASTROBIOLOGIST

When you give up your linear worldview, your playground expands. Things that yesterday seemed irrefutable and impenetrable suddenly open up. You realize that things do not always have to make sense or be explainable through conventional understanding.

On my blog I share stories from readers who have experienced miracles, who have opened to the magic of life. Rarely do these stories come from academia or from scientists, who tend to scoff at the idea that life could possibly offer more than what they can prove in a test tube or a lab.

Dr. Michael Shermer, a professor and public intellectual who writes a monthly column for *Scientific American*, is so wary of all things "supernatural" that in 1992, he started a quarterly journal with the stated aim of debunking fads and cultural influences on science. It's even called *Skeptic* magazine. The avowed atheist once debated the existence of God with Deepak Chopra on *Nightline*.

Which is why I love the following story so darned much.

In the summer of 2014, Michael Schermer married Jennifer Graf from Cologne, Germany. During the shipping of her belongings to his home in California, boxes were damaged, heirlooms lost.

An old transistor radio that belonged to Jennifer's beloved grandfather Walter successfully made the journey. Walter had been Jennifer's only father figure and had died when she was 16.

Michael, knowing how much it would mean, attempted to resurrect the radio after decades of silence. He changed the batteries, searched for loose connections, and even tried what he called "percussive maintenance"—smacking it against a hard surface. He finally gave up, and Jennifer stuck it in the back of a drawer in their bedroom.

On the day they exchanged rings and said their vows in front of his family, Jennifer, 6,000 miles from home, was feeling nostalgic, wishing her grandfather could be there to give her away.

After the ceremony, she motioned to Michael, said she needed to speak to him. Alone.

"There's music coming from the bedroom," she whispered.

Since they didn't have a music system in the bedroom, they searched for errant laptops and iPhones. They even checked the back door to see if their neighbors had unexpectedly scheduled a party.

Michael wrote in *Scientific American*: "[suddenly] Jennifer shot me a look I haven't seen since the supernatural thriller *The Exorcist*."

"That can't be what I think it is, can it?" she said.

They opened the desk drawer and, sure enough, her grandfather's transistor was playing a romantic love song.

The radio continued to play throughout their wedding day. They finally fell asleep to classical music emanating from Walter's radio. It stopped working the next day and has remained mute ever since.

And while famous skeptic Michael Schermer said he'd never have believed such a story if he heard it from someone else, he admitted that "the eerie conjunction of these deeply evocative events" rocked him back on his feet and shook his skepticism to its core.

And that's what I'd call a miracle. That a longtime upholder of scientific orthodoxy was willing to publicly share a revelation that contradicts his aggressively argued position of many years. To actually suggest that science may not be the only road to truth, after all. That it might not offer the definitive and complete view of reality.

At very least, Schermer says, "We should not shut the doors of perception when they may be opened to us to marvel in the mysterious."

PARTY GAME #3

Shake Your Pom-Poms
at Dang Near Everything

"What has trapped you in a belief system that says that your ecstasy can only come when you have certain physical stimuli in place? . . . Ecstasy is your birthright. It is not something that exists outside of you."

— DANIEL SCRANTON, REIKI MASTER

Most people think the *art of allowing* means being open to your Maserati coming, being ready for your perfect partner to show. And they're partly right. When you're on the joy frequency, you're open; you're present; you're working *with* life, not against it. Manifestation occurs instantly in an energy field without conflict.

This game is for those of us whose kingdoms (our consciousness) still have dragons and bad guys. For those of us who still like to whine and moan, who still value the "I'm a victim" booby prize.

True *allowing*, the kind you're encouraged to practice in this game, means recognizing that whatever is in front of you (even if it's a broken-down car, a feisty two-year-old, or a giant tax bill) is something you have called forth, acknowledging that something within you vibrates in tune with this "other."

Rather than take steps to flee or change it, you have to first allow it. You have to bless it. You have to go so far as to call it good. Freedom and power come in choosing to bless with gratitude every single thing that shows up. Anything you refuse to embrace and fully bless imprisons you. It puts up a fence between you and your highest good.

So here's how it works:

Choose to actively "allow" everything that happens, even (and maybe especially) the mundane and ordinary. For example:

- "I allow the morning sunlight to flood through my window."

- "I allow the dog to loudly slurp beside the bed."

- "I allow the water from the spigot to moisten my toothbrush."

- "I allow this minty toothpaste to refresh my mouth."

Practicing on simple things strengthens your allowing muscle. Once you've mastered that, you can pass Go, collect your $200, and begin allowing circumstances that, up until now, you believe wield power over you.

I'd like to thank the Academy, my mother, and my second-grade teacher for this burnt bagel, for this two-hour commute, for the second mammogram.

Cultivate a childlike attitude toward your creations. Ponder them, wonder about them, but most of all love them. That's how you claim dominion over your life.

Behold, I have created this and I call it good.

#S&F
Show us something you used to reject
but now accept wholeheartedly.

The Party Favor: Get on the Enlightenment Fast Track

"Re-examine all you have been told at school or church or in any book."
— WALT WHITMAN, AUTHOR OF *LEAVES OF GRASS*

D-Buzz (the gratitude channel) creates room in your head for the following three Truths:

1. There is nothing you could ever do, nothing that could ever happen, that can separate you from your Source.

2. You are loved beyond anything you could ever imagine. The word *love*, purloined by a culture that knows nothing of the sort, is a paltry substitute for this deep, abiding connection.

3. Because of your inalienable connection to this bigger thing that cannot be named, you have the power to create worlds. In fact, that is why you are here.

The Pudding

"Miracles happen all the time. People just fail to notice them."
— LORNA BYRNE, MYSTIC

Lorna Byrne stared at walls, played with imaginary friends, acted "different" than other kids. Her family was told she was retarded. By the time she was 14, she was pulled out of school. She was diagnosed dyslexic, so her dirt-poor Irish family saw no reason to continue buying schoolbooks and clothes for their "retarded" daughter.

As it turns out, Lorna Byrne was actually a lot "smarter" than the rest of us. She sees things the rest of us miss. Miraculous things, beautiful things.

It wasn't walls she was staring it. She was listening to angels, who forbade her from revealing their presence. *Not yet*, they said.

Her parents, the angels clearly instructed, would commit her to an institution if she told them. The angels had other plans for her life.

To this day, she sees these beings as clearly as we see our children texting their classmates on cell phones. "They are my teachers and friends," she says.

One of her many "imaginary friends" was her brother Christopher, who had died before Lorna was even born. It wasn't until she was 15 that she found out that the rest of her family, caught up in the limited physical plane, believed Christopher had left the planet when he was 10 weeks old. Their strict adherence to conventional reality precluded their seeing Christopher, the angels, and many things that, to Lorna, are an everyday occurrence.

Lorna sees spirals of light, sparkly colors, and waves of energy that the rest of us miss because we've been trained to block out all "atypical" information. She often sees dark energy, for example, in people experiencing illness in their bodies.

Her angels led her to interact with nature, taught her how to see. She grew to love and trust these angelic beings, who often asked her to open her hands to find holograms of stars or flowers made of light. They'd shine and expand from her hand as far as she could see.

Lorna, who grew up Catholic, uses the terminology *angels* to describe the magical entities she interacts with on a daily basis. It jives with her religious beliefs, and it's a

useful word with which most people can identify. *Angels*—
we've all heard of those.

Everything these magical beings ever told her
came true.

Once when she was playing with a childhood friend,
she heard her friend's father, who was far away at the auto
body shop where he worked, calling for help. They ran to
the shop and found him unconscious and bloody, under a
car that had toppled on top of him.

Another time, she saw two young bike riders get hit by
a bus. She saw them continue to ride, peacefully and without a care, on up to heaven even though ambulances and
paramedics were scrambling around the leftover bodies.

When she was 10, one of her angels pulled down a big
screen in the middle of the river. A vision appeared on the
screen of a tall, handsome redheaded boy.

"Remember him," they said. "You will meet him in a
few years, and you are going to marry him, have children.
You will be very happy."

The angel also told her God would take him back to
heaven when he was still young. Not the kind of thing you
want to hear about your future spouse, but Lorna had long
ago learned to trust everything they told her.

When she was 16, Joe, the guy in the vision, walked
into her father's shop and applied for a job. And sure
enough, the two began dating, eventually fell in love, and
got married, just as the angels predicted.

They were also right about Joe's health. After marrying
in 1975 and having four children, Joe got sick and died in
2000. Their youngest child was only five.

After Joe's death, at the angels' prompting, Lorna
went public. Her angels had always told her she would

eventually write books. She just laughed. But she'd also learned to heed their instructions.

At last count, this diminutive, soft-spoken, uneducated Irishwoman has written four books.

She has gone on to appear on BBC, in *The Economist*, and at gatherings all over the world. I met her in London at a Hay House conference.

Even though I write about miracles and magic, I tend to scratch my head when people claim to hang out 24/7 with angels. But Lorna is the real deal.

She is one of the humblest, most unassuming women I have ever met.

I tell you Lorna's story, not to convince you to seek out an angel reading, but so you'll start to unravel your own strict beliefs about what is and isn't possible.

Lorna says all babies see angels and spirits, but by the time they speak their first words, they have "learned" what is "real" and what is not. It is only when we begin to conform to the strict paradigms of our culture that we lose touch with the magical world that surrounds us.

$$\infty$$

PARTY GAME #4

The Loony Goony Game

"We miss the miracle because we're looking for the big boom."
— CONSTANCE ARNOLD, SUCCESS COACH

Be astonished by useless things. It's easy to be thankful for the obvious—healthy kids, public libraries, strong marriages. But in this game we're going to take it a step further. We're going to build our gratitude muscle by also appreciating the insignificant and impractical: the wild geese cutting giant V's in the blue morning sky, the tambourine guy (google him) whose YouTube dancing delights the staunchest of my critical voices, the mischief of weeds that sprout through parking lots . . .

#S&F
Show us something insignificant and/or
impractical that you love anyway.

The Party Favor: Dissolve Static

"I need the memory of magic if I am ever going to conjure magic again."
— ROBERT MCCAMMON, AUTHOR OF *BOY'S LIFE*

When you're on the frequency of joy and gratitude, the universe is free to line things up, work things out, pull rabbits out of hats.

But most of us, instead of staying on that clear, sweet channel where magic happens, hit a bump in the road and immediately start worrying, start dredging up past times when things didn't work out. In other words, we create static.

We create a resonant field that blocks the magical realm where things work themselves out without our input.

Once you tune in to the joy channel, 100 percent of your energy becomes available. You start to recognize every person, every situation, as the exciting and stimulating gift they offer. Once we give up our "lover's quarrel with the world," as Robert Frost called it, energy awakens inside of us.

There's no extra buildup, no white noise, to block Truth. That's when your whole view of life begins to change. People, situations—even your post office box—all start looking different.

And then, once the resistance is dissolved, you get to choose if you wish to continue or start a new adventure.

The Pudding

"One day this will be 20 years ago."

— BILL BRYSON, AUTHOR OF *A WALK IN THE WOODS*

My friend Jay told a story that perfectly illustrates what can happen when we don't create static in our frequency.

He accidentally left his garage-door opener in a rental car. He called the rental agency only to be told the car had already been re-rented. And no, they hadn't noticed his garage door opener.

He could have gotten frazzled. Especially since he was due to meet a friend for lunch and had left his credit card at a bar that wouldn't open for three more hours. On top of all that, his four-year-old son, Emmett, picked that particular moment to pitch a fit.

Jay knelt down, calmly dealt with Emmett, feeling nothing but love and gratitude. Even for the presumed-lost garage-door opener and the credit card he needed to pay for lunch.

"I don't know why, but I just stayed grateful, trusted that all was well," Jay said.

He stopped at his bank to retrieve some cash (since his card was MIA) and there, sitting in the parking lot, was the very car in which he'd left the garage-door opener. An older gentleman was standing beside it, talking on his phone.

Jay asked, "Is that your car?"

"It's my son's. He's in the bank."

Jay explained what happened and asked if he could take a peek inside.

With garage-door opener in hand, Jay got an intuitive hit to go ahead and run by the bar where he'd left his credit card, even though it wouldn't open for a couple more hours.

Sure enough, the owner was sitting outside, also on his phone.

"You're really lucky," he told Jay. "I usually don't get here until three. But I came early today to meet my carpet cleaner."

Jay, of course, knew it wasn't luck. Just further proof that magic is always afoot as long as we don't create "problems" to block it.

PARTY GAME #5

Be a Broken Record

"I say thank you like a crazy person."

— PRINCE EA, RAPPER AND SOCIAL ACTIVIST

Say "thank you" for every single thing that happens. No matter what. Feel free to improvise with *arigato* or *gracias* (see list in sidebar).

No exceptions, exemptions, excuses.

Here's an example.

- *When the alarm clock goes off in the morning . . .*
  "Thank you that I'm here on planet Earth for yet another day."
  (Jim Morrison and Benjamin Franklin, for example, don't have this luxury.)
- *While shuffling to the bathroom . . .*
  "Thank you that I have legs that allow me to move from point A to point B."
  (Go to any VA hospital and you'll find many who don't.)
- *While stirring circles in your Toastie-O's . . .*
  "Thank you that I have ample nourishment."
  (In the time it takes to polish off that bowl, 75 people[1] will have died of malnutrition.

---

[1]   The number 75 is based on you taking five minutes to down a bowl of cereal. If you dawdle and take 10 minutes, we'll have lost 150 brothers and sisters. And in case you're wondering, this is based on stats from the United Nations.

Not only does Louise Hay, founder of Hay House, regularly pull mirrors out of her bra and tell herself how beautiful she is, but she spends a large portion of her day in over-the-top gratitude.

Before she gets out of bed, she thanks her sheets and her pillow. She thanks the sunshine.

She thanks the asparagus and sweet potatoes she eats for lunch.

"I sometimes want to roll my eyes," said David Kessler, her co-author on *You Can Heal Your Heart*. "But she's definitely living in a better world than I am."

Or take it from Jill Bolte Taylor, the Harvard neuroanatomist who, on December 10, 1996, suffered a massive stroke that for eight years stripped away her ability to walk, talk, read, and write. Every morning, she utters a sincere thank-you to her body's 50 trillion cells.

"Every day is precious, a sacred time. I wake up every morning, wiggle my toes and my fingers, and say to my cells, 'Good morning, girls; thanks for another great day.'"

#S&F
Show us something you
blessed today for the first time.

A Thank-You by Any Other Name

Back in my Eurail days, when I was traveling from country to country, negotiating different currencies and mixing up my *gracias*'s and *grazie*'s, I pitched a language guidebook book called *Let's Snow Europe!* The title was a take-off on the popular student travel guide called *Let's Go Europe.*

The idea was to provide English words that sounded like the foreign words you're trying to say:

- *Donkey shoes* for *Dankeschön.*

- *Mares see* for *Merci.*

It probably won't surprise you that I failed to entice a publisher. But here's the next best thing: a guide to saying "thank you" (no fake English words) in 22 languages.

- Arabic—شُكْراً (*Shukran*)

- Chinese (Mandarin)—谢谢 (*Xiè xie*)

- Croatian—*Hvala*

- Czech—*Děkuji*

- Dutch—*Dank je wel*

- French—*Merci*

- German—*Danke*

- Greek—*Ευχαριστώ* (ef-khah-ree-STO)

- Hebrew—תודה (*Toda*)

- Hindi—धन्यवाद/ (Dhanyavaad)

- Hungarian—Köszönöm

- Italian—*Grazie*

- Japanese—がとうございます *(Arigatoo gozaimasu)*

- Korean—감사합니다 *(Gamsahamnida)*

- Portuguese—*Obrigado/Obrigada* (male/female speaker)

- Polish—*Dziękuję*

- Russian—*Спасибо* (spah-SEE-bah)

- Spanish—*Gracias*

- Swahili—*Asante*

- Swedish—*Tack*

- Turkish—*Teşekkür ederim*

- Vietnamese—*Cám ơn bạn*

The Party Favor: Outwit the Crazy Voices in Your Head

"If we saw the world as it really is, we'd be dropping to our knees every five minutes just to say, 'thank you.'"

— THE ZING,
AKA ETHAN HUGHES OF THE POSSIBILITY ALLIANCE

At every moment, you're either living in your natural state . . . or you're not.

Your natural state is joy, aliveness, feeling what I like to call the "Divine Buzz."

It's dancing in ecstasy over the gift of each blessed moment.

Most of us, crazy humans that we are, are clueless to our natural state. We're completely oblivious to our connection to this awesome energy force that is pulling out all the stops to pour blessings onto our heads. We're shuffling along like Eeyore with our "poor me" attitude, never suspecting that we could be celebrating, shouting hallelujah. Never guessing that it's us who barred the door.

The good news is that even though we're unaware of this parallel mystical realm, it can never be destroyed. It's always there, and it will never abandon us.

We don't have to do a damned thing to win its favor. We don't have to pray hard enough or meditate long or really do anything but let go of the mental architecture (begone, you ridiculous posers) we've erected on top of our natural state.

In fact, it's so suspiciously easy to live in our natural state that we refuse to take it seriously. It can't be that simple, we protest.

The Pudding

"Life is so damn short. For f*ck's sake, just do what makes you happy."
— BILL MURRAY, COMEDIAN AND ACTOR

Catherine Behan decided to try a little experiment. For seven years, she has been a practitioner of the law of attraction. She has manifested some vertigo-inducing things—clients, vacations, friends, lovers. But like all of us, she has the voice, that one that asks, "What if this is all bullshit?"

Her brother, a brain scientist at Stanford, was more than happy to represent that part of herself that can't believe life is supposed to be easy.

He constantly called her out: "You can't just have fun all the time. You have to work. You need a job."

Catherine, who has been quite successful running dating websites and offering relationship advice, thank you very much, decided to put her beliefs to the ultimate test.

She posed this hypothesis: If it's really true that the universe loves me and wants me to be happy, wouldn't it make sense to get as happy as I possibly can and let the universe iron out the details?

To test her theory, she decided to get up each morning and do *only* what she wanted. Often that meant walking to the beach with her dog, staring out at the majesty of the ocean. She wrote stories in her journal, visions of a beautiful life, truths she believed in.

For a while, the drumbeat got louder: *You're going to go broke. This is ridiculous. Everybody has to work.*

Her bedroom got messier and messier. The voice (not to mention her roommate) chimed in every morning, "It's getting a little out of control in there."

Still, she refused to budge. She did not want to tidy up her room. And she was committed to doing *only* what she felt like doing.

"Eventually," she says, "I was able to turn down the volume of the old story. I simply focused on finding beautiful things and doing exactly what I wanted to do."

As she began cleaning up—not the room, but the mental debris in her head—opportunities began showing up. The right people began crossing her path. She was invited on a hot-air balloon ride, for example, and an all-expenses-paid cruise. She inherited some money and felt called to attend a workshop in Mexico where "I felt like I was floating on a sea of love."

"It was uncanny," she says. "So many of the stories I wrote in my journal came to fruition, exactly as I pictured them. I feel like Dorothy in *The Wizard of Oz*."

As for that messy room? It eventually became the thing she felt like doing. One morning, she put on some lively music and had a blast straightening up.

"We have no idea of the magic we have inside," says Behan, who can be found at http://ManifestFaster.com.

PARTY GAME #6

Pretend You're on Vacation

"Happier people make a better world."
— GLENNON DOYLE MELTON,
FOUNDER OF THE ONLINE COMMUNITY MOMASTERY

Cultural programming quickly teaches us which activities in life are fun and which aren't.

In this game, no matter what you're doing, deem it fun. Find the joy in it. Pretend you're on vacation.

If Viktor Frankl can find meaning in a concentration camp, I'm thinking those long lines at the DMV could easily be turned into a party.

Attitude is everything. You can either stand there, moaning about a lethargic line, or you can sing "Joy to the World."

Those 15 people ahead of you? They could become your new best friends. Together you could even sing harmony.

So no matter how long the lines get, no matter how demanding your to-do list seems, just remember that "this, too," is an opportunity to revolutionize your life and get onto a brand new frequency.

#S&F
Show us a celebratory selfie.

The Party Favor: Wriggle Out of the Straitjacket of Negativity

"You have to live in your reality,
so why construct it with negative expectations?"

— SHAWN ACHOR, AUTHOR OF *THE HAPPINESS ADVANTAGE*

My daughter, Taz, and I recently took surfing lessons in Santa Teresa, Costa Rica. Our instructor, a Venezuelan named Jesus, was very clear.

"When you get on the board, keep your eyes focused on the sandy beach. Do *not*—under any circumstances—take your eyes off that beach."

"But when do we start paddling?"

"The board," he continued in his sexy Latin accent, ignoring us, "is always going to head toward whatever you're looking at."

Since the last thing Jesus wanted to do was peel two first-time surfers off the scary-looking rocks on either side of the beach, he was adamant:

"Keep your eyes on the beach."

"But when do we jump up, hang ten . . . ?"

"Keep your eyes on the beach."

Jesus's message also comes in handy in life.

When you dwell on what could go wrong, you head for the rocks. When you get all buzzed about how cool something is going to be, you head for the soft, welcoming sand.

When I launched my travel-writing career, I had a choice . . .

I could focus on the rocks:

- *I'm an unknown from Kansas.*

- *I don't know a single person who makes a living as a travel writer.*

- *I have no idea how to get started.*

. . . or I could focus on the sandy beach:

- *It is going to be utterly awesome visiting exotic locales, meeting dashing foreigners, getting begged to stay at five-star resorts.*

- *I mean, can you imagine, getting to write (my favorite thing in the whole world) about countries I've yet to explore?*

When I decided to write a book, I had the same two choices . . .

The rocks:

- *Hardly anybody gets a book deal these days.*

- *Why spend all that time and energy on something that may or may not happen?*

. . . or the beach:

- *How cool is it that I can sit here in my pajamas and do what I love.*

- *How amazing is it that my words can make a difference in people's lives.*

Just like on that Santa Teresa beach, both realities exist.

But the pertinent question is: Which reality is more fun? Which brings more joy?

Why waste the 1,440 minutes we get each day on pessimistic assumptions? Why dwell on worst-case scenarios? Why mentally prepare for doom? Why wait for the dropping of the dreaded other shoe?

Especially when you have the power to focus on how frickin' amazing it's going to be when you find your perfect partner, land your dream job, sign that book contract.

The Pudding

> *"If we learned from suffering, wouldn't*
> *the world be enlightened by now?"*
>
> — JOSH RADNOR, TED MOSBY
> IN *HOW I MET YOUR MOTHER*

When you get happy, when you open your joy channels, the largesse of the universe can't help but rush in.

It's so easy that most people walk right by it, roll their eyes, and think, *Sure, Pam! It can't be that easy.*

So I'll say it one more time. It really *is* that easy.

We have a blast sharing stories in my possibility posse about just this topic. We decided that part of our mission and why we love this group *so frickin' much* is because we take time to register, to note, to document (well, we don't really write it down) how frequently the universe works in our favor.

One week, Frank brought in a stuffed monkey (said he was doing extra credit from Experiment One in *E-Cubed*), Nikki told us about the free pizza she won after taking the day off work, and Rhonda shared the following story that clearly demonstrates the awesome fact that celebrating life brings more to celebrate.

Rhonda and her husband, an architect, went to an awards banquet at a small Catholic college where he's doing some design work. Sitting behind them was a table of eight or so nuns. They were all between 60 and 90 years old, Rhonda estimated.

"Now, I've been to lots of these banquets, and they're always nice, polite affairs. But at this one, after all the awards had been given and the ceremonies had commenced, a DJ came out and started playing dance music," Rhonda said. "My jaw nearly dropped."

And as Kool & the Gang started in with "Celebration," those nuns got up and started dancing. Really getting into it.

"They didn't sit down once," Rhonda said. "And then the emcee got up to pull a name out of the hat for the grand-prize trip to Ireland."

You guessed it?

"Mary Katherine!"—one of the "gonna have a good time tonight" nuns.

PARTY GAME #7

Become a Luck Magnet

"If I don't cheer myself on, who else is going to?"
— KANYE WEST, HIP-HOP RECORDING ARTIST

You don't need a rabbit's foot or a horseshoe. According to Richard Wiseman, psychology professor at the University of Hertfordshire in England and creator of Luck School, people who think they're lucky actually are.

After eight years of studying hundreds of self-identified exceptionally lucky and exceptionally unlucky people, he concluded that getting good breaks has nothing to do with karma or kismet and everything to do with how we see ourselves.

First step in Luck School is to anoint yourself lucky. Wiseman even requires students to sign an official declaration. So today, "audit" Wiseman's class by declaring that you are one lucky son of a gun and that this just might be the best day of your life.

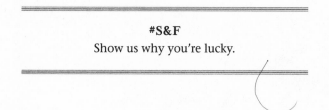

#S&F
Show us why you're lucky.

The Party Favor: Lube the Channels of the World's Beneficence

"Very little is needed to make a happy life;
it is all within yourself in your way of thinking."

— MARCUS AURELIUS, ROMAN EMPEROR

Murphy's law, a famous adage that most of us live by, states that "Anything that can go wrong will go wrong."

I, for one, beg to differ.

It is only our belief in problems that perpetuates the problem. Our constant struggle for awakening is the very obstacle to accomplishing it.

I was on a phone call recently with some readers who wanted to know what my process was. I almost felt guilty because I don't know that I have a "process." I don't have a seven-step solution.

I just know that whenever I am being my mind's bitch, I am not living in my natural state of joy. I am not living my Truth, which is that I am already free and infinite.

Instead of looking for the next teacher, the next book, the next process, I would like to suggest that we spend time following the FP's law that states: "Anything that can go right will go right."

Once we start noticing all that is going right, that is all we will see.

The Pudding

"Absolutely everything is available to us—sorrow and joy,
grievance and forgiveness, horror and transcendence—it's
all on the menu. It's up to us where we put our attention."

— JOSH RADNOR,
TED MOSBY IN *HOW I MET YOUR MOTHER*

Mary Karr, in her memoir *Lit*, tells about her transformation from cynical alcoholic to deep-dyed believer. At first, she resisted all advice from her AA sponsors to pray, to ask for help.

As she says, "No way. . . . Never gonna happen, no offense."

But finally, out of sheer desperation, she uttered something like, "Help me to feel better so I can believe in you, you subtle bastard."

Even after she got a call from the Whiting Foundation, an endowment for emerging writers that awarded her a $35,000 prize she hadn't even applied for, she held tight to her skepticism. It had to be coincidence that the call came within a week of her prayer launch, didn't it?

But the blessings started piling up. The more she practiced gratitude, the faster they came. Even in her writing practice, she began asking the "subtle bastard" to help, which eventually led to her penning *The Liars Club*, a memoir that sat perched on the *New York Times* bestseller list for an entire year.

But my very favorite miracle story comes toward the end of *Lit*.

Mary had just moved her 80-year-old mother out of the teetering southeast Texas hovel in which she'd grown up. Her mother, a gun-toting alcoholic whose lack of parenting skills played a significant role in Mary's life and literary output, started complaining.

An angry confrontation ensued, and Mary found herself lying facedown on the carpet, feeling like an abject failure.

As she began to repeat her prayers, she suddenly remembered the scriptures her spiritual director, a Franciscan nun, had assigned. Because she'd been busy flying across the country to move her mother, she hadn't yet read the verses.

Among her mother's still-boxed books, she found a worn, floppy Bible inscribed to her mother in 1927.

She leafed through the onionskin pages to the first assigned passage, Psalm 51:7–12. The skin on her scalp prickled as she noticed those very verses were marked in pale blue chalk. Her mother, decades earlier, had drawn a wavy line in the margins surrounding them.

How odd, she thought—partly because her mother hadn't been particularly devout, but especially because they were the exact same verses she'd been directed to read.

None of the remainder of the Bible was marked up.

Except when she reached the book of James, which was marked with the same blue chalk.

"This is not the parting of the Red Sea," she says. "This is not a dead friend arisen from his gauze," but nonetheless it is a miracle. That her mother's small hand, circa 1920-something, would highlight the exact two passages Mary would be asked to read 70 years later could hardly be called a coincidence.

As she says, "I know how specifically designed we are for each other. I feel in a bone-deep way the degree to which I'm watched over—how everyone is. . . .

"Every now and then we enter the presence of the numinous and deduce for an instant how we're formed, in what detail the force that infuses every petal might specifically run through us, wishing only to lure us into our full potential."

Building Spiritual Capital

"The earth is drenched in the presence of God."
— ROB BELL, Pastor and author

Practicing gratitude allows us to recognize life at its deepest, holiest level. It opens us up to the realization that everything is sacred. Every moment. Every person. Every *everything.*

Most of us completely miss the life that's throwing itself at us. The life that holds nothing back. Obsessed as we are with our problems and petty annoyances.

As my friend Frank once observed, so preoccupied is he often with his thoughts, Jesus could walk by, glowing and everything, and he'd never even notice.

That burning bush that spoke to Moses? It may have been burning the whole time.

Gratitude enables us to recognize that the world is infused with the presence of something magical, something sacred. Although we make valiant attempts at creating magic (planning big vacations, organizing perfect parties, choosing just the right outfit), the presence of this "something more" often shows up in the most ordinary of moments, in the most ordinary of settings.

I'll never forget the time I was walking across the kitchen. I have no recollection of what I was doing. Maybe taking a dirty dish to the dishwasher. Or checking to see if the strawberries were thawed. Doesn't matter. What matters is that suddenly, I was overwhelmed with a sense of joy, a sense of life and all its fierce beauty. I knew in that moment that no matter what the balance of my bank account, no matter if I got that coveted assignment or not, all was well. Not just "well," but so intensely *beautiful* that if I didn't watch out, I might spontaneously combust with sheer rapture.

PARTY GAME #8

"Back Away from the Dials, Ma'am"

"You can't ride to the fair unless you get on the pony."
— CHERYL STRAYED, AUTHOR OF *WILD*

In this game, no matter what happens, you're going to let the universe go first. You're going to remember that something a whole lot bigger than you is manning the dials. Before assuming anything, before even *doing* anything, you're going to send a shout-out to the infinite, mysterious cosmos. You're going to actually admit you don't have everything figured out.

Yes, you're going to ask for *help*. It's a four-letter word. It's not that hard to say.

If you let it (and you don't even have to say "please"), the bigger thing will gently unravel the candy-coated story that surrounds you and deliver to you the people, the books, the teachers, and the experiences that will awaken you to the truth, the beauty, and the majesty that is life itself.

#S&F
Show us a surprise delivered by the universe.

The Party Favor: Move within Range of the Mother Ship

"When I'm clear, I see only beauty. It's as if my mind were a new solar system pouring itself out in delight."

— GRACE BELL,
TEACHER OF BYRON KATIE'S "THE WORK"

Once you come into coherence with your real Self, a sacred being with no beginning and no end, you can get on with creating beauty and expanding love. You can give up the grasping and the clawing, the pointless plans to protect the linear self.

You are *not* linear. You are light temporarily doing Sue or Bob or Priscilla. I am light temporarily being Pam Grout.

We have become so focused on this transitory, temporal self (the person you call "you") that we forgot who we really are. We forgot how powerful we are. We forgot our true mission—to expand the Kingdom of Light and Love.

The linear self is kinda sweet. It's fine for taking out to dinner, posing for photos, and even posting on Facebook. Spend all the energy you want getting the linear you in tip-top shape. Buy it cosmetics; fix its hair.

But never forget who you really are—God in "drag."

The Pudding

"Thinking of things you're grateful for is the easiest meditation. Do this for five minutes. Then ask for anything you want."

— JAMES ALTUCHER, AUTHOR OF *CHOOSE YOURSELF*

The other day, when I was *not* on the gratitude channel and this book was not flowing as smoothly as I wanted, I put a call out on my blog for stories. I asked if anybody had a great anecdote about gratitude changing their life.

And because the universe gives you anything you ask for, I got the following story from Daniyela, who owns a clothing-design company called Bodhi Designs (www. Bodhidesigns.com).

Like me, she is a single mom and an entrepreneur. Unlike me, she was working really hard. (Sorry, Mom, I know what you said, but I really, really like to play pickle-ball every day.)

Daniyela was feeling fatigued, forgetting to be grateful, and she noticed her energy was going down that road—the one that ends with the haunted house and the screaming children.

Luckily, before she got there and the monsters jumped out, she took a day off. She walked in nature; she mindfully soaked in all the beauty surrounding her. She even did one of my favorite tricks: she started journaling about all her blessings.

"I filled page after page with gratitude, and I could feel the energy shift from a shadowy gray to a bright light," she wrote.

She went so far as to feel elated. She tuned herself in to the Divine Buzz. Which, as any good manifester can tell you, is the *perfect* time to ask for something you want.

She decided she needed a vacation, a *real* vacation where she could unplug, something she hadn't done in years.

But how? she thought. *It's not in my budget.*

When you're on the gratitude frequency, *How?* is a completely irrelevant question.

She put on her abundance shirt (one of the perks of owning a clothing line is you get to sample the products) and went about her day.

Think of a Crock-Pot when making an intention. Put the ingredients in—and voilà! Wait for the tantalizing aroma.

At the end of the day, she got a text from a friend who lives in France. They back-and-forthed for a while, and then he popped the question:

"Do you have any vacation time coming up?"

As a matter of fact, she told him, her daughter was with her ex the first week of August.

"Out of the blue,[2]" she explained, "he offered his air-mile points and use of his apartment. I almost declined, as I felt it was 'too generous.'"

She came to her senses just in time, remembering that the universe had her back, that struggle was unnecessary, and that the only correct answer was *Thank you!*

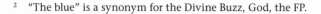

---

[2]   "The blue" is a synonym for the Divine Buzz, God, the FP.

PARTY GAME #9

Get Down with Billy Fingers

"Where would the Jedi be without the Dark Side?"

— JAY HEINRICHS,
EDITORIAL DIRECTOR OF *SPIRIT* MAGAZINE

Billy Fingers, if you haven't read the magical book *The Afterlife of Billy Fingers*, was Annie Kagan's brother, who showed up after his death to prove that who we are transcends the body and exists in all dimensions.

The body/mind you think is *you* is basically irrelevant. It ages. It gets sick. It isn't you. When we came into this material plane, we picked a body—kind of like in the board game *Clue*, where we decide we're going to be Professor Plum or Miss Scarlet. And then we choose a room and a weapon.

This is a game in recognizing how profoundly you color and therefore affect everything you see.

In this game, you're going to get in touch with your cosmic self. You're going to use the ordinary moments of your day to become aware of your naturally expanded, unlimited Self.

Sounds rather woo-woo, I know. But it's actually really easy. Anytime you think of it, let your attention recede from what you see in your viewfinder. Take a moment every so often to notice the outer edge of your field of awareness. *The Way of Mastery*, a channeled spiritual book from the Shanti Christo Foundation, calls it focusing on the shimmer underneath.

We're even going to go so far as to count every disturbance as a blessing. We're going to say "thank you" for everything—especially for things about which we'd normally think, *This sucks.*

Because each time a "This sucks" moment crops up, it's one more chance to embrace it, forgive it, and yes, even love it. Because then and only then, it's free to be on its merry little way.

It helps immensely to appeal to the bigger thing. Here's a prayer I might use:

Okay, FP, here it is again. That damned insecurity—oops, I mean that beautiful part of me that is crying out to be loved. Right now, my reactivity seems to own me. I sure would like to interrupt this long-held pattern. So thank you for giving me yet another chance to finally see the shimmering radiance behind this faulty interpretation. I let it go. It's yours. High fives.

Now go have fun and see what happens!

#S&F
Show us a former "that sucks"
that now shimmers underneath.

The Party Favor: Use X-Ray Vision

> *"The world needs more people who have come alive."*
> — Howard Thurman,
> author and civil rights activist

When you develop an intense interest in seeing Truth and long only to see the qualities of joy, generosity, and peace, the invisible energetic realm is made visible. When you live on the joy frequency—when you shift your vibration to the realm of the miraculous—what longs to be expressed through you comes alive.

You literally animate into your material plane whatever you place your attention upon. When you give your attention to the substance of what's not yet visible, miracles become a daily occurrence.

You say to the universe, "Let me see beauty. Let me see love. Let me see God."

When that becomes all you *want* to see, that is all you *will* see.

The Pudding

"Become committed—fully committed—to the experience of happiness."
— THE WAY OF MASTERY

Be responsible.
Stay on the straight and narrow.
Grow up, for God's sake.
My life is the perfect example of what's possible when we quit fighting and align with the universe.

I'm a single mom from Kansas. Anyone with half a lick of sense would advise me to get a real job, give up my crazy fool dream of being a writer, traveling the world.

My friend Carol, during a slow time in my career, advised, "You should apply at Borders. At least you'll be around books."

As far as I know, that chain of bookstores is no longer standing.

I, however, am doing quite well, thank you very much.

That passion of mine, when I quit fighting life, when I quit believing the voices, provided all the security my mom wanted for me when she suggested I major in the up-and-coming field of computer programming.

We start out knowing magic. We have shooting stars, cosmic universes, whirlwinds inside of us. But then it gets educated away; it gets sent to sit in the corner with the gerbil cage.

People are afraid of our wildness because they're ashamed and depressed they went to work for Borders.

PARTY GAME #10

Decide the Kind of Day You're Going to Have

"I can whine or I can worship!"

— NANCY LEIGH DEMOSS,
AUTHOR OF *CHOOSING GRATITUDE*

The Abraham-Hicks teachings (of *Ask and It Is Given* fame) call this practice *pre-paving*. It's when you pronounce to the world how your day should play out. It's why I gleefully pronounce each morning, "Something amazingly awesome is going to happen to me today." That statement gives birth to the kind of day you desire. By observing (in quantum-physics terms, that means "disturb" or "affect"), you alter the course of your day.

Usually, I give the details up to the universe. I've discovered its idea of awesomenaciousness (yes, it's a made-up word) is far greater, far more beautiful, than anything I can come up with. But if there's something special going on—say, I have an interview or a meeting, doing anything that makes me nervous—I might be a little more specific. Usually my intentions revolve around me bringing my best, most loving game.

A Course in Miracles assures me that unless I make a decision on my own (say, I start feeling down, start blaming the day for not cooperating), that is exactly the kind of day I'm going to have.

#S&F
Show us how you started your day.

The Party Favor: Light Up Your Path

*"The only thing you really want from life is to feel enthusiasm,
joy, and love. If you can feel that all the time,
then who cares what happens outside?"*

— MICHAEL SINGER, AUTHOR OF *THE UNTETHERED SOUL*

If you have Netflix, you'll notice a category called "Because you watched . . ." that lists all the movies or TV shows or documentaries that fall into the same genre. Netflix assumes you'd appreciate these offerings because, well, they're quite similar to options you chose earlier.

Likewise, Amazon recommends books and products that are related to items you've bought and viewed in the past.

This is exactly how the universe works. It continually sends people, ideas, and events that mirror the frequency you emit, the channel you've chosen to speak for your life.

It doesn't charge for these gifts that match what you've previously selected. But it also doesn't discriminate. It doesn't judge or doubt that what you've chosen in the past is what you still want. It doesn't think, *Well, her parents and her culture obviously had it wrong, so I'm going to send her different kind of stuff.*

No. It sends an exact match.

So if you've tuned in to lack, spent your life focusing on what might go wrong, that's what the universe will happily continue to send.

But when you tune yourself in to a new channel, start watching a different type of movie—a movie that brings you joy—you will get people, ideas, and events that mirror the upgraded frequency.

The Pudding

"Freedom can only come to the mind that assumes complete responsibility for the creation of its experience."
— THE WAY OF MASTERY

B. J. Novak, best known for his role as Ryan on the hit sitcom *The Office*, is a stand-up comic, a screenwriter, a director, and the *New York Times* best-selling author of the world's only picture book without pictures. In other words, the classic overachiever.

Unlike many creative types who were urged by their parents to forget their crazy dream, go to law school, Novak always considered a life in the arts as a reasonable career plan. His dad, who ghostwrote memoirs for Nancy Reagan, Magic Johnson, and Lee Iacocca, was a successful writer, his brother a successful composer. It never occurred to Novak that being a writer was an impractical, far-fetched idea.

In college, he wrote for *The Harvard Lampoon* and only days after graduating landed a short-lived writing gig on Bob Saget's *Raising Dad*. He went on to pull pranks with Ashton Kutcher on MTV's *Punk'd*, hone a stand-up comedy career, work with his hero Quentin Tarantino, and eventually win his breakout role as the ever-evolving Ryan Howard.

With a résumé like that, you'd probably suspect Novak to be a workaholic, a slave to his craft. Not so, he says.

The most important component of his success, the thing that best fuels a day of "killing it," is to first get on a joyful frequency. He calls it "powering up" and says it includes looking for an idea that excites him and doing whatever it takes to make himself outrageously happy.

"Being in a good mood is the most important part of the creative process," he says. "But only 100 percent of the time."

PARTY GAME #11

See Trees of Green
(aka The Louis Armstrong Game)

*"You were made and set here to give
voice to this, your own astonishment."*

— ANNIE DILLARD,
AUTHOR OF *A TINKER AT PILGRIM CREEK*

Isaac Luria, a 16th-century Jewish mystic, taught that our job on planet Earth is to raise holy sparks, to lure the light out from beneath the husks. One way to do that is by practicing intense, focused reverence. Give thanks for the one presence that permeates all things.

So in this game, pick a tree and sit with it. As author Anne Lamott says, "trees are so huge that they shut you up." Let "your" tree symbolize the beauty of all creation. Count its many colors and allow its every detail to arouse wonder and awe.

At the risk of sounding like a '60s LSD user, I would also like to suggest you might want to, you know, give your tree a little hug. Matthew Silverstone's fascinating book *Blinded by Science* presents reams of evidence that hanging out with trees improves concentration, eliminates headaches, and even eases stress and depression. Tao Master Mantak Chia, who teaches his students to meditate with trees, says trees are natural processors that release negative energy. According to the Taoist viewpoint, trees, because they've been around for a while, grounded in one place, are able to transmute energy and absorb universal forces.

#S&F

Let's see your tree.

The Party Favor: Taking the Long View

"Magic is becoming the new norm."

— BENTINHO MASSARO,
20-SOMETHING SPIRITUAL TEACHER

When I get an SOS from a reader that goes something like this . . .

"I just don't get it—I gave the universe 48 hours and nada, nothing, zilch" . . .

I want to ask them, "Did you go outside? Did you see the stars? Did you hear the symphony of cicadas that have been hiding below ground for 17 frickin' years, feeding on tree roots and waiting to emerge in a near-deafening crescendo of abundance?"

Sometimes I feel smug, am tempted to *harrumph* at those 1.7 million who wouldn't dream of missing the latest installment of *America's Next Top Model* yet miss the joyful buzz of life right outside their front door. I'm lured into feeling superior to those vacationers who pay big bucks for eco-vacations to "save the turtles" in Costa Rica when they can't even name three plants in their own backyards.

But I can't really point fingers. I, too, often miss the soundtrack of nature. Too often, I'm sealed inside with my windows closed, completely oblivious to the cardinals and tree frogs trilling their advertisements for mates.

I drive right by the mother fox and her twin kits parading beside the road; I miss the squirrel using my fence as a tightrope, the thousands of baby spiders scampering from the sac their mother spun beside my compost pile.

More often than not, it's my smartphone—not the persistent tap of the woodpecker—that wakes me up in the morning.

But oh, those days when I let the magic in. I discover a brand-new episode every hour in my own backyard.

Every morning, the sun rises with a completely different palette of colors, painting a one-of-a-kind vista unique to my GPS coordinates on this big stone hurtling through space. A chorus of birds settles in the trees outside my window, riffing on the day, blaring songs that will never be sung in just that arrangement again.

Every day, we walk by the most remarkable things, things that when we're open, alert, and looking for our gifts can make our knees buckle. The firebush turning sunset red. The ants marching crumbs of a sandwich to the crack in the sidewalk that leads to their colony. The mourning dove making her nest in an outdoor flowerpot.

It's like inhaling God.

The Pudding, Part 1

> *"Celebrate the madness*
> *The joy,*
>
> *Of seeing God*
> *Everywhere!"*
>
> — Hafiz, Persian poet whom I simply adore

Some girls want to be a ballerina or a fashion model when they grow up. I want to be Cindy Ross. I met this larger-than-life dynamo a couple years ago on a travel-writing assignment in South Africa. Among her many accomplishments is having hiked the entire length of the Appalachian Trail, the Pacific Crest Trail, and the Continental Divide Trail, the last with two toddlers in tow. She and her husband, Todd, built their own house—and I don't mean they hired a contractor. They felled the logs, split them, and constructed the entire log house, which sits on the Appalachian Trail, with their own bare hands.

Cindy raised her kids outdoors, and she's writing a book, her seventh, about that journey. It's called *Modeling a Life*. During the 48 hours she was conducting Experiment One from *E-Squared*, she got an over-the-top blessing from Cheryl Strayed, author of *Wild* and a fellow long-distance hiker. The universe was showing off, because during that same time she heard from Richard Louv, whose 2005 *Last Child in the Woods* is considered the bible of outdoor parenting. He, too, agreed to an endorsement.

One night, Cindy couldn't sleep. Her son Bryce was driving late at night to his new apartment in Philadelphia. Thanks to construction on the interstate, the hour-and-a-half trip took nearly four hours. Even after he called to tell her he'd arrived safely, Cindy found herself wide-awake.

She could have lain there tossing and turning, cursing her bad luck for being awake at two in the morning. But she remembered what she calls her "old friends in the sky." She remembered this particular night offered one of the best shows of the year: meteorite showers. She pulled on long pants and a wool sweater and headed outside to the orchard.

The dark patch of sky above her head revealed the Milky Way. Cassiopeia and the Pleiades were hanging in the sky, waiting to welcome her. She clasped her fingers together, tilted her head back, and was rewarded with one, two, three shooting stars.

"Some were so bright and long that I gasped out loud," she said. "They were so beautiful and I was all alone out there with the big sky, performing just for me."

All the worries of her son's drive drained out of her into the earth.

"I focused on what was important. Beauty. That everything was right with the world," she said.

Although she was tempted to return to the house, get a thick comforter, and make a night of it, she began to feel sleepy.

"Just one more," she said . . . until finally, after a dozen meteorite fireworks, she retreated back to her log cabin— but not before one last gift.

A bark from a screech owl saying, "Thank you for joining me this evening."

The Pudding, Part 2

"If you truly love Nature, you will find beauty everywhere."
— VINCENT VAN GOGH, POST-IMPRESSIONIST PAINTER

The old worldview tells us nature is ours to be conquered, ours to exploit.

Thankfully, the more out of touch we become from the natural world, the harder it works to make contact. Like the ignored two-year-old, it's getting louder and louder. It's saying "Hey, you wanna fight? I'll show you. We are one energy. We are one."

The reason I can promise with complete confidence that sometime over the course of the 30-day experiment, you will receive an unmistakable blessing from the natural world is because, at this time on planet Earth, Mother

Nature has put on her dancing shoes. She's showing off and acting out like Miley Cyrus.

Not to step on Alfred Hitchcock's toes, but I'd bet dollars to doughnuts that your blessings might just come compliments of a bird. You know how everybody thinks dolphins have extrasensory powers. Birds, I've concluded, are also in on the action.

Nikola Tesla, who when the world was lit by candlelight, came up with an electrical system that still powers the world today, had a thing with pigeons. A weird thing, where they'd look him in the eye.

Carlos Santana, back in the early '70s, was trying to decide whether or not to become a disciple of Sri Chinmoy, an Indian guru who required certain commitments. The giving up of drugs and drinking didn't deter him, but when Chinmoy asked him to cut his hair and shave his beard? That was a whole different steel guitar.

"Long hair was a mark of honor, my identity," he said.

He was talking with his soon-to-be wife, Deborah, and said something like, "I don't know. I don't want to sound weird, but I got to have some sort of sign."

At that very moment, a bird came swooping into the room, flapped around for a minute, and then flew back out the open window.

"Holy shit," he said. "Did that just happen?"

Deborah turned to him and said, "Okay. I guess you're going to cut your hair."

During the writing of this book, I mentioned the above anecdote and put out the query on my blog: "Has anyone else noticed birds acting as harbingers of the new and exciting world that's being born?"

Within a few hours, I received dozens of stories, stories about birds looking people in the eye, birds bearing messages.

Here's a small sampling.

1. My two kids and I went to the beach to sing a water-healing song and pray for the water. I was wishing I had some tobacco to offer with my prayers. After finishing, I noticed my eldest son coming toward me, following a seagull with something in its beak. As I got closer, the seagull swung around and flew right toward me. I swear it looked right at me as it dropped its package on the ground in front of me. Not only was it a pouch of loose tobacco, but it was the very brand (American Spirit) that I use for my prayers! Can you say mind-blowing?!

2. Two beautiful rainbow lorikeets started showing up right outside my desk window when I began meditating in the mornings about five years ago. Until that day, they weren't there, but now they show up *every single day!*

3. When I was reading and doing the experiments for *E-Squared*, I was deliriously happy, and gift after gift arrived. The most memorable was when 100 little birds arrived at the outdoor cafe table where I was sitting: *Swooom*—they all just zoomed in, landed all around me, like a Disney movie. Yet, the other tables and diners nearby had none. The real joy was the deep feeling of being *heard and loved* and uniquely responded to by the universe.

4. I appealed to my guides for better signs, something that would be completely obvious (yeah, trust much?) . . . realizing that there is some element of faith that's required. I specifically said ". . . and if it's birds,

then I need to see something really special, because I'm tired of looking at every cardinal and wondering what it means." Then I promptly forgot about the whole thing.

The next day, while sitting at my deck journaling, this gorgeous never-seen-before yellow bird sat on a bush right smack in front of me. He stayed long enough for me to take it all in and "get" it, though not long enough for a picture.

I thanked my guides for such a clear sign and went in the house for minute. At that exact moment, my all-time biggest sign started playing on Pandora (it's my go-to, reliable sign from the universe). I was so busy appreciating the booster sign (because my guides were working overtime on my behalf) that it took me a minute to remember the actual song name, "Blackbird," by the Beatles.

5. Joan was my patient, friend, and birding buddy. We started birding together the year she moved away to Texas. She called every May to make plans to go birding on her way out to see her family on Long Island. Last May, I was expecting her to be in touch soon. The next day, her daughter called to tell me she had passed.

That night I was pretty sad, but at the same time felt so lucky to have known her. I even woke up at 3 A.M. and poured my heart into a poem.

A couple of days later, I was telling a friend about one of our last birding adventures. I had promised Joan that I would take her to a well-known wetland called the Basha Kill to see nesting eagles. When we got there, we were unable to access the area because the road was washed out due to heavy rainstorms. Although we were both disappointed, we went to another area of the kill to see what other birds we could find. As we pulled into an open field, we saw a beautiful flash of blue! It was an indigo bunting! It was the most brilliant blue, and Joan was as excited as if she'd won a million dollars! I rarely ever see these birds and we both felt so lucky.

After telling my friend this story, I drove home that day, feeling so happy and grateful for my connection to Joan. Pulling into my driveway, I saw a flash of brilliant blue out of the corner of my eye. As I parked the car, my heart was beating pretty fast. I looked out my window and saw not one but *three* indigo buntings sitting in a row 20 feet away on the neighbor's fence!

6. Birds are showing up freakin' everywhere for me these days. A former and seemingly "very content" agnostic, I've learned that life is a lot "more" than I ever knew before. And birds have definitely been part of the magic.

My favorite bird-cheerleader story, however—and the message is very clear—took place not quite a year ago.

My younger brother, Tim, lost his wife to cancer about eight years ago and has had a tough time bouncing back. Last year, however, he finally made it through the dark and decided to look at boats. Owning and living aboard a boat had been his dream before he married. We looked at a few boats, and nothing "took" until he visited me in Bellingham, Washington, to check out a boat he'd seen online.

It was perfect. I mean, like, *perfect*. It was a perfect setup for living on board. Perfect condition. Perfect price. My brother works at Boeing, where he does test flights on new planes. The boat was called the *Island Pilot*. It was owned by a former career Air Force pilot. My dad is a former career Air Force pilot. And just like all pilots (and especially our dad), the owner had impeccably maintained his craft, kept thorough records and checklists for everything (just like my dad—and brother). The owner was honest, kind—in short, it felt like Tim was buying it from our dad.

I was sold. But Tim wasn't quite there. This was, after all, a big step.

Immediately after looking at the boat, we went to a dockside restaurant for lunch. While waiting, Tim pulled out his smartphone and started reading this article about the top 10 best/worst things about living aboard a boat. "Sunsets," "freedom," and "living more simply" were among the things on the "best" list. He was starting to make his way down the "worst" list. He'd just finished with "no washer/dryer"—which I agreed kinda sucked. Next "worst" item, the author said, was "seagulls"—specifically, having to clean up after them. To which I protested fairly loudly, "Seagulls?! I *love* seagulls!" (I do.)

I swear to FP, Pam, at that moment—literally, within the *second* of having said that—right then!—I was nailed on the top of my head by a seagull in the only way that a seagull could realistically show me love in that moment. :)

I was so damn happy and laughing so hard, I grabbed my iPhone and made my brother snap a pic.

I later heard from seasoned boaters that getting nailed by seagull poo is actually a big-time sign of good luck. :)

Anyway, my brother got the message, bought the boat, subsequently found a wonderful new girlfriend (also a boater), and is living his happily ever after aboard the *Island Pilot*.

PARTY GAME #12

Rearrange the Pie Chart

*"People only suffer because they take
seriously what the gods made for fun."*
— ALAN WATTS, PHILOSOPHER

Let's say something "bad" happens. I put that three-letter word into quotes because it's a judgment call we're not really qualified to make. Nothing is actually "bad" until you pronounce it bad. Nothing merits that descriptor unless you label it that way. For the sake of argument, let's pick a couple of life events that our cultural construct has demoted to the "bad" category. Say, getting cancer or losing your job.

It is standard operating procedure at that point to panic, to call all your friends, to construct horrible endings to the just-revealed news. The triggered "Woe is me" engine starts pumping energy into the utter awfulness of this scenario.

So here's the game. Next time you get a piece of news that doesn't delight you, push the pause button. Let it sit for three days. Or three hours. Know that when the three days (or three hours) is over, you have earned a free unabridged permission slip to throw the world's biggest pity party. At that point, you can cry, beat your chest, write a script for an Oscar-winning horror story.

In the meantime, use the 72 hours to come up with five endings that potentially could make your life better. For example, now that you're free from the old job that—admit it—you didn't really love anyway, you might find a job that's closer to home, that pays better, that utilizes your gifts and talents. I'm not saying you will. But you could. It pays to put energy into the big palette of possibilities rather than to zero in on what your crazy-uncle thoughts want to promote.

My friend Anita Moorjani tells everyone she knows that the cancer that almost killed her was *the* best thing to ever happen to her. The name of her first book, in fact, is *Dying to Be Me.* Her giant tumor demonstrated in living color that fear is manufactured, that she is so much bigger than she thought, and that the universe/life knows what it's doing and she can relax and trust. So much so that Ridley Scott recently bought the rights to her story.

#S&F
Show us the story that Ridley Scott
may just be buying next.

The Party Favor: Put Everything into Perspective

"Let's be unrealistic together."

— A GREETING CARD I SAW AT HOBBS,
THE HOST OF COOL IN LAWRENCE, KANSAS

I have been accused of being unrealistic, a crazy idealist, not in touch with the real world.

"It's impossible," my detractors insist, "for someone to live in gratitude all the time. Sh*t happens."

And I would be the first to agree.

However, 99.9 percent of life, even during the sh*t storm, still operates in perfect working order, continues to run as efficiently as that annoying Energizer Bunny.

Right now, for example, my body is emitting two and a half tons of atmospheric pressure that keeps me from flying off into space. That is a frickin' miracle—99.9 percent of my life is a frickin' miracle.

Anyone who thinks life is nothing but an ordeal is clearly deluded.

For the sake of argument, let's take a count:

1. The skirt you wanted to wear to work is wrinkled in the laundry basket.

2. The freeway is crowded with bozos on their cell phones.

3. Your boss doesn't get you.

And . . .

1. You were created from stars.

2. Free liquid falls from the sky—do you know how remarkable that is?

3. You live on a planet with just the right amount of oxygen and . . .

4. . . . just the right ratio of . . .

5. . . . just the right gases.

6. Each of your cells has thousands of mitochondria that create energy so you can give the finger to me and all the other optimists.

And I'm just getting started.

I'm not suggesting we play ostrich and stick our head in the sands of la-la land.

But why devote so much of our lives to the one-tenth of one percent that isn't working?

Deal with the wrinkled skirt and the boss . . .

And . . .

. . . never forget that your body's 100 trillion cells came from the division of one single cell.

And . . .

. . . that millions of new cells are being born every hour to replace the old ones.

Without, I might add, any input on your part.

Thousands of things have already gone right for you today. So what if your tie has a peanut-butter stain or your seven-year-old refused to get out of bed for breakfast. The vast majority of everything is working with breathtaking efficiency.

Methinks the only responsible position is to use the same pie chart for my life. I choose to divide the 1,440 minutes of my day into the same ratio: 0.1 percent for managing the "sh*t" and 99.9 for celebrating the good, the true, and the beautiful.

It's also worth noting that once I started celebrating the good, the true, and the beautiful, the 0.1 percent became a distant memory.

The Pudding

"Our entire economy is based on distracting us from our blessings."

— GLENNON DOYLE MELTON,
FOUNDER OF THE ONLINE COMMUNITY MOMASTERY

I get a big kick out of noticing events in my life that closely match the beliefs I long held as an anarchist mom, trying to overturn society. One of those subtle frequencies that still shows up every now and again is that institutions are not to be trusted, that *the man* is out to get us innocent individuals who just want to live our lives free from their mendacious tentacles.

Ever since *E-Squared* became a literary phenomenon, my days as a single mom struggling against such forces are over. I now have resources out the wazoo. I always did (so do you), but I wasn't always materially aware of them. I blocked them due to persistent programming that insisted I was all alone, fighting against *the man*.

So I had to laugh when a vestige of that old anarchist belief recently manifested in my life.

Here's how it went down:

My tax advisor suggested I open a SEP (whatever that is) to delay part of my tax burden. At her suggestion, I set up the ability to transfer by phone the specified amount from my checking account to an investment firm (my former enemy, in my old way of thinking). But when I blithely called to do that (even though my advisor verified that it was all set up), I was informed that this was not a possibility. So I ended up having to mail the check by the April 15 deadline. Not a problem, just a slight inconvenience.

Or so I thought.

Even though the package was registered overnight delivery, it didn't show up. And it didn't show up. Finally, my tax advisor ended up transferring the money from my checking account with express instructions to *the man* (aka the investment firm) to mail back the rather large check if it ever arrived.

In June, when I was driving back to LaGuardia on a busy highway, my bank called to tell me I was overdrawn. I knew I hadn't written any checks that could possibly overdraw my account, so I was puzzled.

Turns out, the financial institution, instead of returning my check as promised, ended up cashing it. In other words, I contributed my SEP twice.

My bank quickly corrected the problem, my tax advisor apologized profusely, and the investment firm even offered to send a representative to quell my concerns.

My red-faced tax advisor was adamant. "I just don't understand this. This firm is so reputable. This never happens."

I smiled and explained to her that it was my creation, just a bit of leftover sludge from my former "Down with *the man*" days.

So the reason it may look like the material world isn't matching up with your intentions is because your consciousness is still devoted to old beliefs and expectations. In other words, there's still static in your vibration, still interference disrupting or degrading the transmission you send and receive.

PARTY GAME #13

The Field Guide to Identifying Thoughts and Emotions

"You are not in need of self-help;
you are in need of self-love."

— AMY B. SCHER, AUTHOR OF
HOW TO HEAL YOURSELF WHEN NO ONE ELSE CAN

Most of us believe thoughts just happen. We think we have very little control over our thoughts or the vibratory frequency they emit. This game is intended to call bullshit on this exceedingly popular belief.

Not only is it important to become aware of our thoughts, but it's important to become a Sherlock Holmes at identifying and separating those that inspire us to open up and those we should treat like door-to-door salesmen.

In this game, we're going to get really clear on what various thoughts and emotions do for your frequency. Here's how:

1. Read the following two stories. They're both true. Rate on a scale of 1 to 10 with 10 being, "Man, I can hardly sit here. I'm so excited," and one being, "Oh, was I reading something?"

> **Story A:** A police officer shot and killed a robbery suspect in an exchange of gunfire outside a hotel near Lambeau Field early Wednesday, police said.
>
> "The suspect, a male, got out of the driver's seat with a gun and refused to listen to officer commands.

He started entering the hotel and gunfire was exchanged between the suspect and officers," said Capt. Jody Crocker. "The suspect is dead. The officer's not injured."

That story was copied from a newspaper and, if you're like me, your feeling meter barely budged. You thought, *Been there. Heard that. Got the T-shirt. Guess I'll give it a 1 or a 2.*

Here's the next story, also true, told by a minister to my church.

> **Story B:** A visitor to New York was pulled into an alley by a stranger wielding a gun.
>
> "Here, take my purse," the visitor said to the young man now holding the gun to her head. "You're welcome to it. I know you think you need it. But I love you, and the universe loves you, and you are so much better than this."

The woman, who I'll call Jean because that is not her name, channeled the Bigger Thing. In that moment, she became very clear who she was: love and light. She knew she could never be in any real danger. And most important she knew that this young man was not "the enemy." She recognized a deep spiritual Truth: "Only hurt people hurt people."

She saw that if she were him, if she'd been presented with his life circumstances, she'd be doing the exact same thing.

This is where connection is made. I am you. You are me.

The two of them looked each other in the eye. And then he took off like a scared jackrabbit.

A few hours later, she got a call from the police department. The young man had turned himself in, surrendered her purse. Not only that, he later tracked the woman down at the address he'd copied from her driver's license. He said he'd come to apologize and to tell her that her complete lack of fear had changed him at a deep gut level. In short, she loved the crime right out of him.

Now, I don't know about you, but that story makes me happy. It gives me hope. It furthers my belief that we really aren't separate and that one person does make a difference. I'll give it a 10.

Pop quiz question #2:

2. This set of stories, both true, comes from the Syrian refugee crisis. Again, rate how each makes you feel on a scale of 1 to 10.

Story A: On ABC's *This Week with George Stephanopoulos,* the Republican front-runner called for surveillance of U.S. mosques and the creation of a database of Syrian refugees.

"We have no idea who these people are," he said. "When the Syrian refugees are going to start pouring into this country, we don't know if they're ISIS, we don't know if it's a Trojan horse. And I definitely want a database and other checks and balances. We want to go with watch lists. We want to go with databases."

The GOP candidate said he's skeptical of statistics that show most of the Syrian refugees flooding into Europe are women and children.

"When I look at the migration and the lines and I see all strong, very powerful looking men, they're men, and I see very few women, I see very few children, there's something strange going on."

I give this story a 1, because it makes me sad; it drives a wedge between me and a brother whom I would much rather love.

Story B: While watching news footage about Syrian refugees arriving in Greece, Cristal Logothetis, a California mom, noticed all the young moms and dads pouring out of boats carrying children too young to walk.

When she saw the viral photo of the young Syrian boy who drowned as his family was trying to reach safety, she thought, *Wow! That could have been my son.*

Rather than throw her hands in the air, as we so often do, Logothetis threw herself into action. She began collecting baby carriers.

She started a Facebook page called "Carry the Future" and found thousands of people eager and excited to help, even attaching notes of encouragement and love to the donated carriers.

After she'd collected a mountain of baby carriers, even more than she expected, she joined 10 other moms and headed to Greece to meet families coming off boats, to teach the already-stressed parents how to use the donated carriers.

"More than anything," Logothetis said, "it meant a lot to these families to know that the world wants to help.

"People really care. They do. They just need the right opportunity to get involved. If everybody does something, no matter how small or big, we could make a positive impact on this planet."

Okay, so which of the two stories made you feel better?

It's important to identify how these stories make you feel and to realize that you are the one who decides what kind of stories to feed the circuitry in your noggin.

#S&F
What new story are you
feeding into your brain?

The Party Favor: Take Off the Brakes

"Thought is the Play-Doh of the universe."

— MICHAEL NEILL, HAY HOUSE SUPERCOACH

When I was a kid, Mattel came out with an electric hot plate (it was called a ThingMaker) for creating rubber Creepy Crawlers. All you had to do was pour plasti-goop into a die-cast metal mold, heat it to 390 degrees, and— voilà—you had a whole rubber arsenal of spiders, ticks, beetles, cockroaches, toads, snakes, and even miniature octopuses.

That's what our thoughts do. They take the rich substance of the universe and mold them into physical things.

Thoughts, by their very nature, are inventive. Right now, whether you're aware of it or not, you're using the electromagnetic power of your thoughts to create.

If you make an intention without being on the joy frequency, you apply the accelerator and the brakes at the same time.

We're taught a certain way of perceiving the world, and that is exactly what shows up. Yes, we might make an intention to have more love in our lives, but when we believe—and *have* believed ever since Simon Fitzroy rejected us in seventh grade—that it's a rare phenomenon, that it's something we have to track down and lasso, then we attract *that* reality, not the intention we began affirming on Tuesday.

When you live in gratitude, you no longer create accidentally or incidentally. You invent your life and all its many components from the goop of pure love.

The Pudding

> *"I believe reality is a marvelous joke staged for*
> *my edification and amusement and everybody*
> *is working very hard to make me happy."*
>
> — TERENCE MCKENNA, ETHNOBOTANIST AND AUTHOR

There are two magic words I use continually when I need to remember that we're making this world up. That material reality is nothing but a product of our perception. And that at any time, we can change our perception and change our world.

I learned these words when I was in Rotterdam from, believe it or not, a fabulous 29-year-old who healed her body after a near-fatal scooter accident. For five years, Natasja Frowijn was bedridden, in excruciating pain. When doctor after doctor told her she would live the rest of her life in a wheelchair (if she was lucky), she was ready to take a boatload of morphine and call it a life.

But instead, she decided that she would heal herself—not for her family, not for her husband, but for herself.

"I decided that that not only would I heal myself, but I would go on to live an awesome life," Natasja told me.

She appealed to her grandfathers on the other side. She said to the universe, "Show me."

That day, she "just happened" to turn on *Oprah* (yes, Oprah is also popular in Holland) and saw Louise Hay talking about how she healed herself from cancer. Natasja had never heard of Louise Hay, but that was clear enough guidance. She was on her way.

That week, a woman knocked on her door offering an eight-week course on Louise's *You Can Heal Your Life.* From that moment on, Natasja has been able to draw into her life pretty much every thing she ever wants. For her, it's a game.

Today, she's completely healthy and whole. She works part-time as a nurse and part-time as a medium, talking to folks on the other side.

She's beautiful and fabulous, and I'm so grateful I was able to meet her.

As we were talking, I thought, *Wow, this girl should write a book*, and guess what? She has already started. Not five minutes later, a publisher came up and said she wanted to see her book. Although Natasja is holding out for Hay House (and, believe me, if Natasja wants it, it's as good as a done deal), I was amazed by how quickly she drew this to her. Many people spend decades trying to attract a publisher.

So you're probably wondering, *What are the magic words?* Don't let their simplicity fool you. The words are *It's okay.*

No matter what. No matter what is happening to you, it's important to acknowledge that "it's okay."

No matter how you feel, "it's okay." No matter what you think, "it's okay."

Most of us, instead of being "okay" with our lives, get all balled up with judgment and fear. We exhaust ourselves trying to make things different.

The loving intelligence, the big quantum playground, knows exactly how to play out in our lives. But when our little pea brains get involved (*Oh no! I shouldn't feel this way. I must stop this now. Kick-kick-kick. I'd better call my friends and hash this out. Or join a support group, start a blog*), we put out a murky energy that blocks the healing current.

Our thoughts emit an electrical charge. And when the thoughts are busy "not being okay," we put up a roadblock to our good.

"It's okay" is the energy of love. So whatever is happening in your life, simply say, "It's okay," and let the loving flow of the universe do the heavy lifting.

Amplifying Creative Capital

"Everything around you . . . was made up by people that were no smarter than you. And you can change it, you can influence it, you can build your own things. . . . Once you learn that, you'll never be the same again."

— STEVE JOBS, CO-FOUNDER OF APPLE

In my TEDx Talk, I gave the audience a creativity test. Like the MCAT, which measures suitability for med school, and the LSAT, which screens for law school, my test offers a score.

It has one question:

- Are you breathing?

Here's your score:

If you answered "yes" to this very important question, that means you are highly creative.

So the real question is, *Are you willing to bring forth the gift that only you can give?*

That's where creative capital comes in.

Party Game #14

Write a New Story
That Makes You Happy

"Doubt the default."

— Adam Grant, professor at the Wharton
School of the University of Pennsylvania

If you saw *Sliding Doors*, the 1998 dramedy starring Gwyneth Paltrow, you'll remember it alternates between two parallel universes, one based on Paltrow's character, Helen Quilley, catching the London Underground, and one where she misses it. The two universes yield completely different outcomes.

So in this game, take a story that makes you unhappy and create a parallel universe that jibes with the theme of gratitude and joy.

Here's mine:

The story: It's really hard to revise a manuscript.

The backstory: Because I'm a seasoned writer, I tend to turn in clean copy. Other than a couple typos and a few exaggerations, my specialty, editors usually like my first drafts. This book, in fact, is the first requiring a major overhaul. My neurochemistry is preaching at me, telling me it's hard to revise a book. Upon seeing my editor's notes, my wiring immediately groaned and thought, *This is going to be a major pain in the ass.*

The parallel-universe story: So, knowing that my story is one of many in the field of quantum possibilities, my task is to rewrite this story to one that makes me happy, excited. One that amps up my neutrinos.

First, do I absolutely know it's going to be hard? How could I possibly know that? And then using Byron's Katie's third question from her four-question "The Work," I ask myself, *How does that thought* [that it's going to be hard] *make me feel?*

It feels horrible. It makes me scared. It makes me retreat, procrastinate, choose to do anything but write. So obviously that's not a thought I want to "water," a thought in which I want to invest.

So what is a thought that better serves me? What are some thoughts that nurture what I really want?

How about a story revolving around how much fun this rewrite is going to be, about how much better and more useful the book will become. What if adding all these actionable steps (or in this case, party games) ends up being the most fun thing I've ever done?

Evidence to support that story is plentiful. I already love to write. I've got notebooks full of ideas. And it gives me one more chance to send out even more molecules of love and joy.

To borrow Prince's moniker, I call this rewrite "paradise formerly known as problem."

#S&F
Show us a bread crumb from your new story.

The Party Favor: Invite Blessings to Fall in Your Lap

"A miracle is an invitation into a new story."

— CHARLES EISENSTEIN,
AUTHOR AND ALL-AROUND INSPIRING THINKER

When you completely trust the universe, throw yourself into its loving care, you know every single thing that happens has the potential to catapult you into greatness. Especially things we have a tendency to judge.

I do not *want this.*

I would never *choose this.*

Except you did. For the same reason golfers make pilgrimages to the challenging Cyprus Point golf course at Pebble Beach. For the same reason Sean Penn took roles as a vicious murderer, a murdered gay activist, and a mentally challenged father. For the same reason I seek out pickleball matches with players far beyond my ken.

We all want to expand our game. And the sooner we can say, even if through gritted teeth, *I choose this . . . I want this*, the sooner we can get on with using the 0.1 percent as the vehicle to expand the universe.

The Pudding

*"Miracle stories are helpful, because
they help us question what is."*

— RAM DASS, AUTHOR OF *BE HERE NOW*

After years of success as a freelance writer, publishing 15 books and securing regular writing gigs for such name brands as *People* magazine, *Travel + Leisure*, and *Bridal Guide*, I ran into what, at the time, seemed like a huge catastrophe.

It was 2009. A constant stream of bad news about the recession dominated the headlines. My profession, journalism, was among the hardest hit. Many of my colleagues in the newspaper business were given pink slips. Publishers were cutting back their lines, lowering their advances.

In the past, I always said, "Talk to the hand" to anyone preaching doom and gloom, but this time it hit my pocketbook. Nobody, it seemed, needed my writing services. I couldn't seem to sell another book. Or even many articles. The kiss of death was haunting my life as a freelance writer.

Until I remembered: A recession (and my participation in it) was only one of ten million (or more) possibilities. It was but one of the infinite number of superpositions in the quantum soup.

A *superposition*, in the quantum world, is when particles are still waves, dancing around in countless states, countless positions, and countless possibilities. They all have different energies and frequencies and move at different speeds. It isn't until they are measured, or chosen—as I chose them when I sashayed through the "Ain't it awful" alley—that they coalesce into one material reality, thus destroying the original configuration where all is possible.

At that point, I had little choice but to give it up to the universe. It was so obviously apparent that I couldn't do it on my own. I fell to my knees (actually, I think I was standing) and begged, "Okay, big guy. You're the CEO of my career. I'm currently failing miserably. I need to know whether or not to give up this crazy dream. Should I get a job?"

Which probably was all I needed to say. But *no!* I wanted to complain.

I went on: "I'm raising a daughter here. On my own. She's going to college in a couple of years. I'm in my 50s. I have no retirement. I'm feeling a little insecure here. A little scared. What in the heck am I supposed to do?"

And then I heard this voice:

I didn't support you all these years as an independent freelance writer just to drop you on your ass.

As always, you have a choice. You can continue to flip out. As you've noticed, you'd certainly have lots of company.

Or . . .

You can take a few deep breaths and remember that you are so. much. more than a 50-something worrywart.

Admittedly, your freelance career screeching to a halt is certainly one of the possibilities. It's even kind of interesting, in a soap opera–ish sort of way. It smacks of drama, it garners sympathy from your inner circle, and it's a synchronistic backstroke, right alongside the majority. For once, you're not the odd man out.

But c'mon, Pam, is this really where you want to join the herd. Really?

I love ya. And I wouldn't be myself if I didn't let you choose your experience. As always, you get to decide what matters to you.

But here's one more possibility to throw in the mix. Remember that verse in the Bible that your dad used to preach, the one that says "Ask largely"?

Did you forget about the invisible laws that govern the physical universe? Did you forget you are a child of the most-high God?

Taz is only a junior in high school. Do you really want to decide now that you are going to be poor when she's in college?

Or do you want to subscribe to the Infi-net (as opposed to the Internet, where you're reading all the bad news), where all things are possible?

What if you let go of the fear and the anxiety? What if you choose to relax, to get on the frequency of gratitude, to let the bigger thing rearrange things for you?

I gulped and said, "Okay!"

I focused on developing a different operating system, a broadband channel over which blessings could more freely flow. I worked on the internal circuitry that had shorted out by reading the headlines.

My main tack was to channel Joseph Campbell. To follow my bliss. To move toward the things that makes me feel most alive: writing and traveling.

I accepted as many travel-writing gigs as I could with *The Huffington Post*. Most of my professional writer friends bristled at the idea of contributing to this online sensation that was one of few places still scooping up content by the shovelfuls.

"How could you?" They'd look at me with abject disgust. "They don't pay. *Huffington Post* is for the likes of Alec Baldwin and Marlo Thomas, people who don't need money."

While admittedly, HuffPo didn't solve my financial dilemma, it fully solved my "What do I want to do when I grow up?" question. As I've always said, I would do this even if I didn't get paid.

I happen to *love* writing. I *love* traveling. So rather than sitting at home, twiddling my thumbs and waiting for magical opportunities, I threw myself into what I love.

I wrote dozens and dozens of travel articles for *Huffington Post*. I wrote about castles in Prague, festivals in Montreal, bars inside baobab trees in Limpopo, South Africa. As I like to say, I opened my joy channels.

One day, I came home from a run and found a message on my answering machine from a guy named Joe Littell. He was from Fallbrook, California, and said he had written a novel and needed my help.

I figured it was probably some crank. When you're a writer, it's more or less impossible to get into a conversation without the other half of the dialogue informing you they have a great idea for a book. But what the heck? Other than the exciting trips to far-flung climes, my professional work schedule at the time was as free as the bird in Lynyrd Skynyrd's famous song. I called the mysterious stranger back.

Turns out, Joe Littell was a legit person who had started a wildly successful textbook company in Chicago. After selling it to Houghton Mifflin in the '80s, Joe retired to California with his millions. The reason he was calling, he said, is because he just happened to be a fan of *Kansas Curiosities*, a book I'd written seven years earlier about quirky characters and roadside oddities in my home state.

Hardly a contestant for national bestseller lists, the book had done quite well in Kansas. My local library even chose it one year as the Read Across Lawrence book, buying dozens of copies to disperse to anyone who wanted to participate in the yearly program.

But how did a guy in California who I'd never met and never even heard of run across a copy?

Joe was full of fascinating tales. He'd lived all over the world as a missionary's kid; he'd gone to an Ivy League school. And now he wanted to know if I'd be interested in reading (for pay) his novel set in Kansas. He wanted to know if I'd edit the book, add my Kansas expertise to "spice it up" a bit.

"Let me check my calendar," I said, my heart pounding loudly.

A few weeks later, some VP for the American Automobile Association (AAA) called to see if I'd be willing to teach a webinar about my National Geographic book *The 100 Best Vacations to Enrich Your Life*. All I had to do was get on the computer and answer questions.

Um, yeah!

And from that point on, I went back to putting my faith in the invisible and infinite flavors in Campbell's quantum soup.

PARTY GAME #15

The Opposite Game

"What we have chosen to see often costs us true vision."
— *A Course in Miracles*

Remember this popular childhood game, where you state everything backward?

To wit: "This ice cube is so hot." Or "Megan Fox is so ugly." Or "I don't like you very much," which, of course, means "You are everything to me."

It works like a charm when people spout unhappiness, inanities, and misinformation. The opposite game helps me realize they're simply replaying old tapes and need my love. It helps me not to take everything so personally and to remember what I call the biggest secret in the world—that we all really love each other.

My friend Diane tried this tactic with the IRS. Instead of reacting with fear and distrust, she called the auditor assigned to her case with great enthusiasm.

"I'm really excited about our meeting," she said, purposely treating him like a long-lost friend.

Not only did the surprised auditor nearly drop the phone, but he responded in kind. Their meeting ended up being a big joyfest.

Or consider Julio Diaz, a social worker from the Bronx who was approached by a teenage boy with a knife. He gave the boy his wallet, and as he scurried away, Diaz yelled after him, "Hey, wait. It's cold out here. If you're going to be robbing people for the rest of the night, you might as well take my coat."

It threw the boy off his game, so Diaz continued, "If you're willing to risk your freedom for a few dollars, then I guess you must really need the money. I was just going for dinner, and if you want, you could join me."

Gandhi, who learned to make sandals in South Africa even though he was an attorney, made a pair for the General Jan Smuts, the South African general who imprisoned him. When asked why, he replied, "He's just as much a hostage to the system [of apartheid] as I am."

Radical actions such as these might seem small, but they upset the dominant apple cart. They create a resonant field that goes out and makes our world a little sweeter, a little safer, a little more beautiful.

#S&F
Show us something from
your overturned apple cart.

The Party Favor: Find the Gateway Drug to Abundance

"Laugh and play and love and dream beyond all reason, and miraculous things begin happening."

— MARTHA BECK, AUTHOR OF
FINDING YOUR WAY IN A WILD NEW WORLD

D-Buzz is causative energy. Feeling grateful—being on the joy channel—attracts magnificent things into your life. When you're grateful, you become a magnetized rod pulling in the iron filings of all your desires.

When you're bitching and complaining, you repel the good.

By noticing even one tiny thing you like about an unpleasant situation, you can grow it into a supersize reality. Like a lettuce seed, it starts small, but can grow into big, leafy, nourishing greens.

Being grateful makes things happen. It's the seed, the gateway drug.

Unless, of course, you prefer to operate under a framework that insists manifesting takes hours of visualization, years of self-flagellation.

You are already connected to everything in the universe. You have already "created" everything you desire. It's already there. It's a reality. It's just that you're focusing more on the way it "appears to be" than on the reality you want to see.

Gratitude junkies with clear, unsullied frequencies can bring whatever they choose into the material plane with the snap of a finger. Look at Jesus and those multiplying fish and loaves. He turned five loaves of bread and a couple of fish into a feast for thousands.

Sathya Sai Baba, a holy man from southern India, was able to pull lockets, rings, and other jewelry out of thin air. I know what you're thinking. But it's that very thinking that creates the static. Anything you cannot believe possible will never *be* possible for you.

I'll let Erlendur Haraldsson, professor emeritus of psychology at the University of Iceland, make my case. This distinguished scholar, who has published in many prestigious journals, studied Sai Baba for ten years. He wrote a book, *Modern Miracles*, about his investigation, and while he readily admits he cannot prove there was no mass hypnosis or sleight of hand going on, he saw (with his own two eyes) reams of evidence that the materializations Sai Baba had been manifesting since he was 14 were the real deal.

In one instance, Sai Baba was explaining to Haraldsson how daily life and spiritual life should "grow together like a double *rudrasksha*." Haraldsson, who had never heard that word, asked what he meant. Neither Sai Baba nor the translator could come up with an English equivalent, so Sai Baba merely closed his fist, waved his hand, and then opened his palm to reveal an acorn-like object growing together like a twin orange or twin apple.

Sai Baba then said, "I want to give you a present," and held the object in his hands. He blew on it and the double seed was suddenly covered with a gold shield and attached to a gold chain. On the top was a cross with a small ruby. Not only did Haraldsson later discover that double rudrakshas are rare botanical anomalies, but a London goldsmith who inspected the necklace verified its gold was 22 carats.

While this kind of manifestation rocks the very foundation of our current worldview, it's not uncommon in India.

Sai Baba frequently handed out jewels and other costly objects made of gold. He was also known to materialize fruit, fragrant oils, and grains of rice with perfectly carved images of Krishna.

Haraldsson could produce no evidence these feats, which had been occurring for more than half a century, were not genuine and, as he says, a testament to "the enormous potentialities that lie dormant somewhere within all human beings."

So the question is, *Do you want to manifest your desires now, or do you want to continue believing you need more time?*

The Pudding

> *"To believe there are difficult or unreachable*
> *things, doesn't change the nature of those things.*
> *It only changes our position towards them."*
>
> — DANIEL MARQUES,
> RESEARCHER, POLYMATH, AND AUTHOR

I'll let Roland, a reader of *E-Squared*, tell this story, which created quite a stir when he shared it on my blog. Take it away, Roland:

> I was talking to a friend, Gary, on the phone while surfing the magazine *YachtWorld* and looking at sailboats. He suspected I was not totally present and asked what I was doing. I admitted that I was looking at yachts and wished that I owned a 38-foot Catalina and could have it slipped in the San Francisco area with the freedom to fly out, cruise, and just hang.
>
> Minutes later, I spotted a 38-foot and asked Gary to hold on while I checked it out. It was exactly what I envisioned, and as I read on, the owner said he would be willing to trade for an inland boat (quite unusual) and that he would trade for a 32-foot Catalina, which is exactly what I owned.
>
> I got off the call with Gary and called a Salt Lake City number. No answer, so I left a message. Half an hour later, I noticed the Salt Lake number on my phone and returned the call.
>
> "I called a Denver prefix. Are you in Denver?"
>
> "Yes, are you in Salt Lake?"
>
> "I live there, but I'm in Denver today on business."

He asked to see the boat, and I told him the boat was not in Denver but currently stored about 50 miles north by the Estes Park exit.

He said, "I'm north also and very close to that exit."

Now I'm thinking, *No way,* and, *This is getting a little weird.* I told him who to contact, to check it out, and, if interested, to call me back.

He called back, said he loved it and wanted to trade! At this point less than an hour had gone by, and I'm thinking, *Wow, even the universe can't move that fast.* (Not.)

At this point I was scrambling and trying to figure out how I might wiggle out of this; we had not talked numbers yet, so I figured that would be my way out. I offered a ridiculously low figure, and he said, "Great, when can we close the deal?"

PARTY GAME #16

Do the Happy Dance

*"It doesn't matter how strong the
broadcast is if your receiver's turned off."*

— ESTHER HICKS, CO-AUTHOR OF *ASK AND IT IS GIVEN*

Wanna know one of my most important spiritual practices?

Erupting into spontaneous dance. In places besides dance floors.

Here are five reasons it's as important as meditation:

1. **Dancing cuts thought off at the knees.** All spiritual practice is about getting out of our own way, letting go of all thoughts that block the Divine Buzz. The majority of our thoughts are boring reruns from yesterday, the same ole to-do lists, fears, and gripes.

And the Truth is that life works just fine without our incessant input. In fact, the more we distract the yammer, the better things actually work. This may seem counterproductive, but your right and perfect path will show up once you quit trying to figure everything out. It's all the figuring and fretting that keeps it away. Dancing shuts down the mind so Truth can emerge.

2. **It puts you on the same wavelength as the FP.** As I'm fond of saying, you can't watch ABC if you're tuned in to NBC. When you're joyfully dancing, you're on the same channel as the Big Guy. Which, of course, makes it easier

for the FP to pour out all those countless blessings with your name on them.

3. **It makes other people happy.** I spend a lot of time in airports. And for the most part, the thousands of people waiting for flights are doing the same thing: staring at their cell phones. One day in the Cincinnati airport, my daughter and I spotted (well, there was really no possibility of missing him) this tall, gangly young man dancing jubilantly through the terminal. By himself. We were sitting at a Chick-fil-A (this was before I began boycotting them) when he zoomed joyfully by. We both began laughing, and like the young children in the German fairy tale "The Pied Piper of Hamelin," we began to follow him.

And who can forget the wonderful scene from the movie *The Full Monty*, where out-of-work steelworkers began tapping their feet in a dance routine while waiting in the unemployment line?

4. **It heals your body and eliminates other ailments.** My friend Betty is 82. Most of her peers, when they get together, discuss one thing—their health, or lack thereof. What she discovered when she took up dancing was that the conversation (between fox-trots) became elevated, and people forgot all about their health issues. They actually started having fun, feeling young again.

5. **It jars you into a new reality.** Worldview 2.0 is all about ditching ruts and mental architecture that squeezes us into a tiny, uncomfortable box. Worldview 1.0 includes dancing, of course, but once we're grown up, it occurs only when there's alcohol and a dance floor. By dancing in places where others don't expect it, we jump out of the box, and our consciousness can't help but follow. Again,

THANK & GROW RICH

life forms around our beliefs and expectations (our consciousness), so the more we can expand our beliefs and expectations, the bigger toehold life has to flow in.

#S&F

C'mon! We want to see your moves.

The Party Favor: Sprinkle Fairy Dust

"Be in love with your life. Every minute of it."

— JACK KEROUAC, BEAT GENERATION AUTHOR

Amy Poehler tells a funny story in her memoir, *Yes Please*. She has a thing about the moon, describes herself as a "moon junkie." Not only does she track lunar cycles on her iPhone, but she regularly takes her two young boys moon hunting. On these excursions, they wear pajamas (makes it seem like they're breaking out of jail), carry flashlights, and eat moon candy, which, as she says, "looks suspiciously like M&M's."

One full moon, after buckling them into the backseat, throwing in the sleeping bags (for lying on the ground and howling), and driving furiously to get to her chosen open field, one of her sons said, "Mama, it's right there. We don't have to drive to the moon. It came to us."

That's pretty much the trick to life. If you settle down, get happy, and tune in to the joy channel, the moon, the stars, and every good thing in life will come to you. The principle I talk about in my books isn't called "the law of working your ass off." It's called the law of attraction. As in beckon, lure, magnetize.

The work on our part is minimal.

The Pudding

*"My only three goals in life: (a) I want to be happy,
(b) I want to eradicate unhappiness from my life, and
(c) I want every day to be as smooth as possible."*

— JAMES ALTUCHER, AUTHOR OF *CHOOSE YOURSELF*

In the 2001 Pixar hit *Monsters, Inc.*, two lovable monsters, employed by "the man," power their city (called Monstropolis) by scaring sleeping kids and downloading their energy of fear. It worked like a charm until those monsters, Sulley and Wazowski, accidentally discover that laughter creates ten times as much energy.

Turns out, it wasn't just a silly movie. We can change energy fields by being in joy and spreading love. That may sound like a small thing—changing an energy field. But indeed, it's the framework for all that exists. Although the energetic realm is invisible, it permeates everything and affects everything. All of us are in on the game.

Every time we love, we create energy. Every time we laugh, we create energy. Every time we choose to forgive instead of hold grudges, we dismantle the illusion that we are separate beings, living a separate existence.

James Altucher, a successful entrepreneur and author of many books, tells a funny story about the day he saved the U.S. stock market. It was March 9, and, as he says, everything was going to hell. The S&P 500 was heading toward a 20-year low after a decade of Internet busts, corporate corruption, a housing bust, bailouts, Madoff, and other miscellaneous downers.

So he did the only thing he could think to do.

He bought a bag of Hershey chocolates and stood outside the entrance of the New York Stock Exchange passing them out. Even though people were staring at their feet like zombies, everyone stopped, looked up, took the chocolate, and smiled.

First of all, chocolate releases phenylethylamine, the same hormone that gets activated when you fall in love. So for a brief moment everyone was a little happier, a little less depressed.

In other words, Altucher changed the energetic frequency of Wall Street. Laugh all you want, but by the end of the week, the S&P was up nearly 75 points.

Party Game #17

Wear Your Freak Flag

"When you try to be safe, you live your life being very, very careful, and you may wind up having no life at all."

— Byron Katie, author of *Loving What Is*

In this game, you're encouraged to do something that scares the bejesus out of you. Break one of the unwritten laws of acceptable human behavior.

Tim Ferriss, in his best-selling *The 4-Hour Work Week*, encourages people to lie down on the floor in a public place, count to ten, and then walk away like nothing happened. It's not illegal. Or morally wrong. Pretty much anybody has the equipment to do it. The only problem is it violates one of those many unwritten laws mentioned above.

We follow these laws every day, all the time, as if our lives depend on them. On those rare occasions when we step outside the box, mostly because we f*#ked up or, in this case, because it's recommended in a self-help book, we learn that nothing can really hurt us.

Nope. That didn't kill me. Nope. Neither did that.

Stephen Colbert calls it "loving the bomb," a concept he learned from an improv coach at Second City, the iconic Chicago institution where he launched his comic career.

"It took me a long time to really understand what that meant," Colbert said in a *GQ* profile. "It wasn't 'Don't worry, you'll get it next time.' It wasn't 'Laugh it off.' No, it means what it says. You gotta learn to *love* when you're failing. . . . The embracing of that, the discomfort of failing in front of an audience, leads you to penetrate through the fear that blinds you."

Colbert says he trained himself to steer toward fear. All of us are scared of each other, scared to appear foolish, scared to do it the "wrong way."

Colbert's spiritual practice (although he may not call it that) was to purposely embarrass himself in public.

While the rest of us were meditating and beating pillows, Colbert was boarding elevators and singing really loud. He did things that were socially unacceptable, things that taught him, *Hey, it's only my crazy mind that could think there's a problem.*

"The feeling you feel is almost like a vapor. The discomfort . . . comes around you," he says.

You want that moment to end. *Now!*

But when you breathe it in, move toward it instead of heading the other way, you transcend. Right there in the elevator with all those people looking at you.

So, when things appear to be going wrong, give yourself a fist bump, say, "thank ya, Jesus," and run toward them like they're George Clooney giving you bedroom eyes.

#S&F

Let's see your freak flag!

The Party Favor: Override the Bald-Faced Lies

"Gratitude is an opener of locked-up blessings."

— MARIANNE WILLIAMSON,
AUTHOR OF *A RETURN TO LOVE*

The universe leaves bread crumbs. Like Gretel in the fairy tale.

But when you're on the wrong frequency, you walk right by them. Like trick-or-treating in a sheet. You can't see a damned thing through the holes.

But it's not fair. Wrong frequency.

He has more. Wrong frequency.

I'm tired. Wrong frequency.

Keep twisting that dial until you get on the frequency that prompts you to pump your fist in the air and shout, "Bring it!"

The Pudding

> *"Thank you is the best prayer anyone could ever say."*
>
> — ALICE WALKER, AUTHOR OF *THE COLOR PURPLE*

"You're doing what?"

When my friend Cheryl Miller told me she was moving to Overbrook, Kansas, to start a health-and-wellness center, I thought she was bat-sh%t crazy.

Her home in Lawrence, just down the street from me, was gorgeous, *Better Homes and Gardens* gorgeous. Why would anyone in their right mind choose to leave? Especially in favor of a town that, on a good day, might claim a population of 1,000, most of whom have never even heard the word *wellness*, let alone *yoga*.

But Cheryl had no choice. She lives on the gratitude frequency, and life sprinkles fairy dust for her to follow. While she was building her Fairchild Wellness Retreat, weird things[3] happened. A carpenter knocked on her door right when she was in the market for shelving. The 10 beds

---

[3] Again, another synonym for God

she needed for the retreat center showed up . . . at a craft store. While I was there, finishing up this book, Cheryl, on her way to the chiropractor, found three bicycles in a field of bicycles.

"It popped in my mind that the center needs some bicycles," she told me, "and *boom*, there they were! For $3 a piece."

You can't get a bicycle horn for $3. And who finds a whole field of bicycles next to sorghum and wheat fields?

You're probably thinking *coincidence*, but this kind of thing happens to Cheryl . . . all . . . the . . . time.

"People look at what I've done [turned an old historic home into a peaceful oasis], and they think, *Man, that's a lot of work. You're retired. How can you possibly work this hard?*"

Cheryl just smiles, because she knows there's very little work involved.

Rather, she comes up with an idea (usually sent by the universe) and then sits at her pagoda with a beer or a cup of coffee (depending on the time of day) until the thing she thought of shows up.

The rest of us call this miraculous. Cheryl calls it life.

But it wasn't always this way. Cheryl used to be depressed. Life, as far as she could tell, sucked the big one.

Until the year she decided to consciously upgrade her frequency. Someone gave her a string of Tibetan prayer beads. She made the commitment that every night for an entire year, she would write down a blessing for each of the 110 beads. First couple nights, she'd reach 10 or 12 and hit a wall. But she persisted. Eventually she came up with categories:

Things I'm grateful for that I don't have to do, for example. Or *Things I like about my job*. Or *Things I like to eat*.

"Now," she says, "I could write a thousand blessings every hour."

Without even realizing it, Cheryl hooked into the Divine Frequency where life is simple and joy prevails.

PARTY GAME #18

Impersonate Wonder Woman

"I could feel energy exploding out of his head."

— GARRY SHANDLING,
STAND-UP COMEDIAN, ACTOR, AND WRITER

In other words, use physiology to change your brain. Acting happy, regardless of how you actually feel, coaxes your body into dumping a whole lot of feel-good drugs into your brain.

If you've seen Amy Cuddy's TED Talk, you already know that standing like Wonder Woman generates confidence. I do it before all my talks. I often ask my audience to join me.

Scientists have proven that standing with your fists on your waist and your legs spread in what Cuddy calls a "power pose," lowers your cortisol and boosts your testosterone. Two minutes is all it takes to ace job interviews, tests, and other potentially stress-provoking events.

So in this game, whenever you get testy, simply slip into the bathroom (Superman's phone booths are practically obsolete these days); strike a Wonder Woman pose; and come out, if not in cape, a whole lot calmer and happier.

Another strategy is to grin like a lunatic. Researchers discovered that positive brain activity is stimulated when human test subjects (I guess the rats weren't cooperative) force smiles for as little as 20 seconds. Hewlett-Packard researchers, using an electromagnetic brain-scan machine and heart-rate monitor, found that smiling stimulates happy brain chemicals equal to 2,000 bars of chocolate or getting $25 of unexpected money.

#S&F
You guessed it—it's time to show
off your Wonder Woman pose.

The Party Favor: Open a Vast, Yet-to-Be Imagined World

"There is only one rule on this Wild Playground. . . .
'Have fun, my dear; my dear, have fun.'"

— HAFIZ, PERSIAN POET

Gratitude creates space for something new. It creates room for healing to occur, intentions to show up, miracles to happen.

When you limit yourself to what you already know, what is already here, you block your inheritance of infinitude. Instead of using the vast, multidimensional palette of possibility, you zero in on what you've been taught.

Here's one example:

Let's say you want a new car. Because there's a standard process for getting a car (choosing the one you want, visiting dealerships, chatting up car salesmen, taking out loans), you forget that's one of a bazillion potentialities. Instead of focusing on the fun you'll have driving the new car, instead of getting psyched about the hotties who will beg to ride in it, you start working, you start zeroing in on the standard process.

That negates the field of infinite potentiality that is your inheritance.

Every structure that you've been taught (for example, the process for getting a new car) is only one interpretation—it's only one potentiality.

When you open up—make space—you find there are literally thousands of ways to get a new car. You could win one. A friend of my daughter's won a fully loaded maroon SUV at a graduation party. Someone could unexpectedly give you one. A reader of *E-Squared* said a former priest whom she hadn't seen in years gave her a car, no strings attached.

The point is, the less you absolutely know for sure (rigid structures that block other possibilities), the easier it is for the field of infinite potentiality to work its magic.

When you create space in your consciousness, you create an opening for something new to occur.

Match.com is not the only way to meet a man. Calling a realtor is not the only way to find a new house.

The Pudding

"Kick this day in its sunshiny ass."

— GREETING CARD I SAW AT
THE THIRD PLANET IN LAWRENCE, KANSAS

Rob Brezsny was driving along an LA freeway, not exactly a chapel for spiritual development. He merged into a lane in front of a hot blonde in a Jaguar who under any other circumstances might have been worth a second look.

But in this instance, she was *not* happy. She laid on her horn and gave him the international peace sign minus the forefinger.

Probably wasn't an unusual occurrence on the morning freeway, but she refused to let it go. She kept glaring and honking and making it clear to everyone that Rob was an asshole and that she had been wronged.

Rob, who prides himself in being a wise, loving human being, got hooked. He took the bait, and before long he and the hot blonde were in an angry cat-and-mouse game that would have interested the camera operators of *Furious 7* had they been available that morning.

Except Rob didn't feel good. His pulse was racing; his heart was pounding; his adrenaline was screaming, *Kill the threat!* The creator of my favorite horoscope normally speaks for peace and love and international understanding.

So just in the nick of time, before a car accident or something even more dire, he asked for help from the Bigger Thing.

Suddenly, an overwhelming truth hit him. He realized the bottom line: "I love this woman." He waved and sent her this message that is true for all of us: *I love you. I have always loved you. I will love you forever.*

He said, "I don't know if she felt it or not, but I want to believe that she got the energy and that she was as changed by that realization as I was."

∞

Expanding Adventure Capital

*"Waving my gratitude like a flag is . . .
what keeps the gift in motion."*

— AMANDA F*CKING PALMER,
PERFORMANCE ARTIST

Life is supposed to be fun. Some of you will have to take my word for it.

Most of us were trained that life will be fun:

- Someday.

- If you work hard.

- On the weekends.

- When you retire.

No one bothered to mention that life should be enjoyed *right now*. All the time.

Instead, we were taught to be careful, to rein in our enthusiasm, to use our quiet voices.

God forbid that you would slurp your soup. Or talk to strangers. Or take off your pants and run around the neighborhood.

In fact, we were told that most of life *isn't* fun, but that's okay because there are enough fun times to make up for the nonfun times. In fact, we are taught that if you devote yourself to enough nonfun times (working hard at school, slaving away on your degree), you will someday earn the fun times.

Nobody told you that if you follow your joy, you'll accomplish great things.

As Biz Stone, co-founder of Twitter, says, "The most important quality of any job is that it's fun. I knew Twitter would eventually work where the other start-ups didn't (yes, he had plenty of failures before Twitter) is because it brought me joy."

Even the $500 million offer for acquisition from Mark Zuckerberg (he and partner Ev Williams turned it down) came because they were joking around. When driving out to the Facebook office for what they knew would be an offer to buy them out, they agreed, on a whim, to ask for something so big that he'd never go for it. "Let's ask for half a billion," they laughed.

Sure enough, Zuckerberg called a few weeks later offering that very amount.

Party Game #19

Where's Waldo?

"[I] lie down and . . . let everything buzz around me."
— Alicia Vikander,
Academy Award—winning actress

Go on a scavenger hunt for five things you've never noticed before.

According to a study in *Science* magazine, we humans spend 46.9 percent of our waking hours thinking about something other than what we're doing. Mind-wandering is a cognitive human achievement, no doubt, but when the nonpresent pervades our mental lives, our happiness decreases.

According to the Harvard psychologists who conducted the study, "where our minds are is a better predictor of happiness than what we're actually doing."

This is a game of awareness, a game for discovering the glory of the present, a game that can turn wherever you are into hallowed ground.

When I play this game, I am flung back to the beauty of this moment. I once again realize all the beautiful things that have been here all along. I become a reviewer who can't help but give my life five stars.

~

The other day I was walking my dog (lots of things happen when I walk my odd-looking bassador—that's part basset hound, part Lab) by a railroad track. It's junky, not exactly a spectacle for the eyes. I've walked this route countless times. But earlier that morning I'd been reading *Blue Iris*, a book of poems and essays by Mary Oliver. Most were about flowers.

In about three blocks, next to what many would describe as an eyesore, I found at least seven species of teensy little flowers. Teensy little flowers that I'd undoubtedly marched by many times and never noticed. I plucked one of each and pressed them between waxed paper and into a big, heavy book. I figure they'll be a good reminder next time my ego decides to launch a new campaign around lack and fear.

They aren't the big, showy blossoms florists stock, but each one is ridiculously beautiful, and I am embarrassed that I walked by so many times without noticing.

#S&F
Show us one of your "new" things.

The Party Favor: Shout "Bring It!'

"The mother of excess is not joy but joylessness."
— FRIEDRICH NIETZSCHE, GERMAN PHILOSOPHER

Everything you're trying to manifest is already yours.

This is important to say again. *You already have everything you want.* Otherwise, you wouldn't know you want it.

All of it is sitting right there in your field of potentiality, twiddling its thumbs. But because you're on a different wavelength (the wavelength of "I don't have it," the frequency of "I'd better get on my running shoes and move faster, try harder"), it's still invisible to your senses.

Each of us is already living the life most extraordinary (on one of the FP's channels), but because we're focused on all we don't have or on what we're trying to get, it's fuzzy and not something we can put our hands on. It's surrounded by static.

Just like a filmmaker decides which of many objects his lens focuses upon, we get to decide if we want to zero in on the stuff in the foreground (what we have now), or if we prefer to shine our lens on something else. We're the camera operators.

Reality is not static or complete. It's an unending process of movement and unfoldment. We choose what to unfold, what to put before our lens, where to shine our spotlight.

The Pudding

"Love allows you to transcend the great fear, the great suffering that comes from a temporary, mistaken identity problem."
— THE WAY OF MASTERY

Rainn Wilson studied acting at NYU and lived in Williamsburg before Williamsburg was cool.

"My clothes were thrift shop, not because I was a hipster, but because that's all I could afford," he says.

He drove a moving van to squeak by and went to every audition he could. Five times, he auditioned for roles on *Six Feet Under*, a popular HBO show following the funeral home of the Fisher family. Each time, he was overlooked.

"As frustrated as I was at the time that I didn't get cast as Tommy, gay choir member number three, I now couldn't be more grateful," he says. "You never know what the cosmos has in store for you and sometimes repeated rejection is simply . . . preparing you for something greater."

The universe, apparently, was waiting for the perfect role on *Six Feet Under*: Arthur Martin, the yogurt-loving intern from Cypress College of Mortuary Science, the role that changed Wilson's life forever.

Party Game #20

Maro Up

"Piglet noticed that even though he had a very small heart, it could hold a rather large amount of gratitude."

— A. A. Milne, author of *Winnie-the-Pooh*

I learned this game from Ken Honda, a successful Japanese author who has written more than 100 books. His popular seminars sell out in less than an hour. I was blessed to meet him and appear on his widely heard podcast when recently in Japan.

After our interview, he gave me a little wooden box with a gold coin. It was a gift from his mentor, Wahei Takeda, a billionaire investor who is spending his final years (he's 80-something) giving and spreading joy.

Mostly, he's sharing the powerful technique he used to become Japan's wealthiest man.

It's not what you think.

Every day, Wahei "maros" up.

Maro is short for *magokoro*, which means "true heart." It's rather hard to pin down or define, but it's a spiritual state of unconditional love for yourself and others. According to Wahei, it radiates an energy that draws good fortune into your life.

In order to maro up, Wahei says *"Arigato"* (Japanese for "thank you," you might recall) hundreds and even thousands of times a day. He believes there's great power in this one simple word and that saying it, appreciating even the smallest things, oomphs up a person's ability to attract great things in their life.

He calls gratitude a multipurpose tool, like a Swiss Army knife, that helps people fulfill their destiny. He's such a believer in the magical power of "thank you" that he created the now-famous Arigato baby cookie. While factory workers make the healthy, potato-based biscuits, a recording of kids singing a happy "Arigato" song plays over the loudspeakers. Wahei believes it makes the workers happy, which in turns puts positive energy into the cookies.

Wahei claims maro is the key to his success. When you come from the frequency of pure joy and gratitude, you radiate love, which in turn attracts miracles—and money—and creates win-win situations for everyone. Saying "thank you" over and over makes you appreciate the sheer miracles of being alive.

Wahei's philosophy boils down to this: *If you love the world, it will love you right back.*

So maro up today by saying "thank you" as many times as you possibly can.

#S&F
Show us you loving the world.

The Party Favor: Recruit the Voice in Your Head for a New Job

> *"Happiness is where you start from rather than where you go. God, I sound like Yoda."*
>
> — SIMON PEGG, ACTOR

Self-help books always start with a problem. An author defines an issue—say, not having enough money or having too much stress or clutter—and then proceeds to tell you exactly how to overcome whatever problem he or she just convinced you you have.

This book is just the opposite. It starts with the premise that you have absolutely no problems and that it is only your insistence on identifying problems and then working really, really hard to overcome them that makes them seem real.

Notice I said "seem."

Most problems are manufactured and don't even exist until we begin looking for them.

But even worse is that once you start believing you lack something, you fail to appreciate all you already have.

You fail to notice the blessings that pour down on you like sunbeams on a golden summer day.

It's like locking yourself in solitary confinement.

Fans of *Orange Is the New Black* know that the "shoe," or SHU (which stands for Special Housing Unit), is a solitary cell where you're sent when you talk smack to a guard or get caught smuggling in heroin or lipstick or Snickers bars. Being in the SHU can drive you crazy. Sitting all alone in a barren cell. Nobody to talk to. Nobody to share the pain.

It's metaphorically where we end up when we forget we're connected to this big wazoozle of a cosmic force that runs the planet.

The Pudding

"God is my boo."

— Maya Angelou, poet and author

While I was giving a playshop (my name for what most authors call a workshop) in Seattle, an intuitive consultant named Maleah Jacobs handed me a book called *The Gratitude Jar*. While it would be deliciously fun to tell you she just psychically intuited I was writing a book on gratitude (and who's to say—maybe she did), the fact remains I had mentioned my new book the Friday before.

Either way, I loved *The Gratitude Jar* and knew immediately it deserved a shout-out in *my* book. It's Exhibit A in my argument that gratitude is causative energy.

This short little book was written by Josie Robinson, a former school guidance counselor who leaned toward alcoholism and depression. After her boys were born, she plummeted fast, smiling on the outside but miserable and out of control on the inside. She finally hit bottom at a friend's surprise birthday party, where she slurred her way through small talk, shouted obscenities, and stumbled over furniture.

The next day, for the first time in a decade, she dropped to her knees and prayed.

"Hey, God! I know it's been a really long time . . . I need your help. . . . Just take it over. Everything. . . . Hit it, God. I'm ready."

Three days later, after a string of events that some call coincidence (not us—we know better), she met Maleah. Her sister-in-law, doing some marketing work for Maleah's busy Seattle practice, gifted her with a healing session with the intuitive/spiritual coach.

Not only was Maleah able to read (over the phone, no less) exactly what was going on, but she offered concrete suggestions for dealing with what Josie called her "dysfunctional life." Among other things, she instructed Josie to start a gratitude jar. She told her to jot down blessings, daily wins, and "synchronicities" to serve as reminders that the universe was conspiring for her good. She recommended sticking with it for 30 days.

Josie, who had more or less run out of options, took the idea to heart. Every night, right before bedtime, she and her four-year-old son, Lucas, mulled over their blessings and added them to the gratitude jar, which was actually a *Star Wars* Easter basket.

Long story short, all the things that were going wrong (not having enough money, disappearing friendships, not having enough hours at work, overdrinking, and so on) disappeared.

"I quit thinking about all the things I needed to make me happy—being thinner, richer, whatever else—and instead focused on everything I already had," Josie writes.

Not only is she still sober today, but in the course of planting the seeds of gratitude, she lost 20 pounds (simply by changing from thoughts of hating her body to finding reasons to be thankful for it), found her dream job, and moved into a house in one of the nicest neighborhood in her hometown. Today, she says, miracles follow her wherever she goes.

"Before the gratitude jar, I didn't know how to escape the black hole I'd fallen into. Now being grateful is the default setting of my brain. Who knew that life is so downright extraordinary. Gratitude pulled me out of the darkness into the light."

PARTY GAME #21

Channel Your Inner Six-Year-Old

*"I'm no longer sure what the question
is, but I do know the answer is yes."*

— LEONARD BERNSTEIN, COMPOSER

There's a reason J.C. said, "Let the children
come unto me."

Kids know important stuff, stuff we mature adults
work very hard to unteach them. Today, instead of urging
your children to "be careful" and "act responsible," you
should follow their lead.

Here's how:

1. **Make believe.** You don't have to tell a kid that "anything is possible." They're pros at "pretend," or what behav-
ioral specialists call *visualization*. Olympic athletes, in fact,
spend nearly as many hours mentally rehearsing their success as they do physically practicing. *Well, duh?* our kids
could tell us. They don't need anyone's permission to be
a pilot or a doctor or an architect. They're already flying
around the room and healing their dolls' boo-boos and
building sand castles. They know Popsicle sticks can be
boats, batons, or bridges over moats. Or better yet, lined
up all the way to Bulgaria.

2. **Ask, "What's the hurry?"** If you want to expand
your world, go on a walk with a four-year-old. Their world
is endlessly interesting. There's no such thing as a bad anything. They notice the sun glinting off the mud puddle.

The snail making figure eights of slime along the sidewalk. The hawk perched on the neighbor's mailbox. Sure, you know everybody's Facebook status. But preschoolers? They know everything else.

#S&F
Show us your beautiful four-year-old self.

The Party Favor: Open Door #1—The One with All the Prizes

"Life is short. Love is vast. Live like there's no tomorrow."
— MICHAEL ROBOTHAM, AUTHOR OF *LIFE OR DEATH*

Olivia Pope, the beautiful protagonist on popular TV political thriller *Scandal*, is what's known in Washington, D.C., as a fixer. Her company of "gladiators in suits" work overtime to mitigate and avert a wide array of crises.

Thankfully, our personal issues lack the same political ramifications, but that doesn't stop us from being every bit as devoted to crisis management as Ms. Pope. The average adult, I'm told, spends 73 percent of his or her waking moments fixing things; planning for things; attempting to prevent things, worrisome things, from happening.

Instead of getting personally involved in our problem, we can just as easily let go and let the majesty of the universe do its glorious thing.

The tactic of aggressiveness sometimes works, but it employs "weak energy," an energy that will always play second fiddle to the simple power of willingness, of gratitude, of trusting in life.

Gratitude brings openness, flexibility, new possibilities. It's the prerequisite for change. It's always the starting point for manifesting goodness.

The cultural norm says:

- *You have to fight for what you want in this world.*

- *Nothing comes easy.*

But there is another way.

When you cultivate a grateful mind, you come from a place of power—you unlock an energy that unifies, that encourages wholeness.

Yes, this energy is invisible (making it a lot harder to trust for some folks), but it's far more tangible and powerful than forcing and grunting and groaning will ever be.

When you get on the gratitude frequency, you can step back and allow it all to unfold with ease and grace.

The Pudding

"If I ever had to create tenets for a spiritual path to healing, number one on my list would be to make sure to laugh as often as possible."

— ANITA MOORJANI, AUTHOR OF *DYING TO BE ME*

Consider Mozart. During his short 35 years, Wolfie, as his friends called him, wrote more than 600 pieces of music. Many, like Tchaikovsky, who called him "the musical Christ," believed his music was divinely inspired.

Mozart himself was the first to admit: "I have no idea whence and how these ideas come."

But he knew he couldn't force them.

To be blunt, Mozart was a big kid. He loved games; he had a propensity for bathroom humor; he was a master at card tricks. He played billiards and charades and kept many pets, including a starling that could sing a theme from his own Piano Concerto no. 17. He loved to dance and play pranks on friends.

In short, he followed his joy. He played around and allowed the universe to use him as its secretary.

His composing was effortless, unburdened. Rarely, if you look at his scores, did he ever mark a note out or change anything. It's as if he downloaded it straight from the Divine. Which could be why his music still resounds with lightness, joy, and elegance today.

PARTY GAME #22

Thank Your Possessions

"We are here on Earth to fart around.
Don't let anybody tell you different!"

— KURT VONNEGUT, AUTHOR AND FAMOUS WISEASS

I learned this little game from Marie Kondo, whose book *The Life-Changing Magic of Tidying Up*, encourages people to appreciate their belongings.

For example, say . . .

- . . . to your clothes: "Thank you for keeping me warm."

- . . . to your accessories: "Thank you for making me beautiful."

- . . . to your shoes: "Thank you for helping me stand proudly in front of my co-workers at today's presentation."

Kondo suggests treating your belongings as if they are alive. She has been known to pull out her cell phone just to admire and appreciate it. As she points out, our possessions work hard for us. They support our lives. Plus, as an added bennie, clothing that's loved, she says, lasts longer. Of course, some people scoff at the idea that inanimate objects respond to human emotion.

'Course, they'd never convince most baseball players, who make deep, intimate bonds with their mitts. Tigers catcher Bobby Wilson, for example, slept with his mitt, took it to school every day for five years, and introduced it to his wife as his "first soul mate." Torii Hunter, who won nine Gold Gloves, gave his gloves names, likened his relationship with each to dating. Former Oakland A's coach Mike Gallego, also a former utility infielder, was so attached to his Rawlings RYX glove of eight years that he risked his life to rescue it when the 1989 earthquake shook San Francisco's Candlestick Park.

#S&F
Show us your favorite possession.

The Party Favor: Windex the Window of Your Awareness

"Go for good and all that's not the truth of you will fall away."
— MALEAH JACOBS, SEATTLE INTUITIVE

Problems are blessings with mistaken identities.

Every disturbance is one more chance, one more scratch-off ticket with the winning prize of "letting go of scripts and games."

It's not that we're bad people. We're conditioned people, innocents playing conditioned roles, reading conditioned scripts, mercilessly judging our performances.

When we tune in to the frequency of gratitude, we come down from the stage; sit in the audience; and rather than judge (gratitude is incapable of judging—it's too pleased and content), we simply observe. Gratitude simply practices awareness.

We might still be regurgitating our scripts (*I'm a failure, I deserve more than this, I'll never get what I want*), but instead of composing scathing reviews, we simply watch and appreciate how robot-like we are. Sometimes we can even laugh.

When you're in the frequency of gratitude, you're never judgmental, because you realize that failure is an impossibility. even remotely an option. No need to solve problems. You're simply practicing awareness.

The Pudding

> *"The good in the world isn't just my hallucinogenic*
> *optimism. How do you like that? Science!"*
>
> — BIZ STONE, CO-FOUNDER OF TWITTER

Biz Stone, who went from college dropout with massive credit-card debt to wildly successful entrepreneur worth $250 million, saw his role at Twitter as being "the not-worrier."

"When everything's wrong and broken, instead of harping on what's wrong and broken, find what works, and build on that."

He says the solution always emerges if you look for the positive.

Biz throws around words like *infinite possibilities*. He knows attitude is everything and that we pull from the quantum field a match to our beliefs and expectations.

As he says, "For any one problem, there are infinite potential solutions."

Creativity, he argues, is limitless. If you cling to what you know, you miss out on the limitless possibilities.

When Biz was unemployed and living in his mom's basement, he printed business cards touting, "Biz Stone, Genius." He claimed to be "building inventions with infinite resources and a world-class team of scientists" at his headquarters—naturally titled Genius Labs. It was his pronouncement of this dream that brought it into reality. He knew to focus on the end result he desired.

That same visualization launched his career at Google. He determined he wanted to work there, and even though he had no college degree (Google typically restricts their employee searches to Ph.D.'s), he visualized his way in. He says he saw it clearly in his mind's eye before it came true.

"I'd manufactured this opportunity without a college education, much less a higher degree; without working my way up a ladder. . . . I wasn't a shoo-in; I wasn't anything. But I did have experience in one particular area: creating my own opportunities."

When he started Twitter, he visualized that it would eventually "topple despotic regimes," which, as we all know, it famously did in a revolution in Moldova and then again in what we now call the Arab Spring.

As he says, hard work is important, but success is more about looking through the "lens of infinite possibility."

Here are three other things I absolutely adore about this leader, who knows the invisible realm always provides the blueprint for the visible.

1. He recognizes that money doesn't make a person happy. Sure, he's now worth a quarter billion, but he and his wife, Livia, live simply and give most of their money away. "Our version of buying a Lamborghini and owning a giant house is that we give away a lot of money to help others," he says.

2. He hired a corporate social responsibility employee before he hired his first salesperson.

3. He envisions a radically different business model. Rather than profit being the end-all-be-all, his mission for any business includes the following three prongs. First and foremost, it should make a meaningful impact. Second, anyone who gets involved (i.e., is employed at said business) should *love* what they are doing; and third, it should generate strong revenues. That's the *third* priority.

He also knows how to turn failure into "the best thing that ever happened" and that together, we, as a motley bunch of optimists, can change the world.

Enlarging Social Capital

*"Stop being boring and show the
world what awesome looks like."*

— ROBBY NOVAK, YOUTUBE'S KID PRESIDENT

What if every day we saw ourselves as powerful radio towers for joy, for love, for connection?

What if we adopted the attitude: "I am light, and I stand before you to love you."

What if we took responsibility, within our own frequencies, for cleaning up toxic environments? What if we decided to emit goodness, to spew beauty?

So what if you don't have the resources to be a philanthropist. As you will see in the upcoming games, financial jackpots are only one (and not even the best one) of the resources in your portfolio. You can smile at people. Make conversations. Start up trivia contests in lines at the coffee shop. Make it your task today to emit molecules of happiness to every person you come in contact with. Make it your mission to uplift everyone you see.

Approach them with this attitude: "I have been waiting to meet you all of my life."

PARTY GAME #23

Save a Life Today

"He contained a whole universe that I had yet to know."
— PATTI SMITH, SINGER, POET, AND VISUAL ARTIST

Pick the biggest palooka you know (works best when this lout is not a friend or family member) and see if you can get them to smile. Rhonda picked the husband of a friend, whom, well, nobody liked that much. Instead of avoiding him like everybody else, Rhonda decided to take him on as her personal project. She decided to see only love. When she talked to him, she'd treat him as if he was her best friend.

It took a while, but . . .

"Like magic," she says, "he eventually changed."

You don't have to transform the whole world. Just your little piece of it.

#S&F
Snap a selfie of you and your new bestie.

The Party Favor: Stack the Odds in Your Favor

"The only way to deal with an unfree world is to become so absolutely free that your very existence is an act of rebellion."
— ALBERT CAMUS, PHILOSOPHER

You have been trained to be unhappy.

You have been trained to look for problems.

You have been trained that what you have now is not enough.

On the joy and gratitude channel, you realize none of it is true.

Countless scientific studies show that steeling yourself against the negative, preparing for the worst, actually puts you on a trajectory heading straight for the very thing you're hoping to escape.

In study after study, Barbara Frederickson, psychology professor at University of North Carolina–Chapel Hill who researches the impact of positive emotions, discovered that feeling groovy affects our biological and cellular makeup; improves our relationships; and enables us to better activate a full range of intellectual, social, and emotional resources.

When you give the floor to the negative internal voices, your physiology bumps into fight-or-flight mode, which might make you run really fast, but suffice it to say, does *not* make use of your full potential.

Running from saber-toothed tigers, both real ones and imaginary ones, completely blinds you to possibility.

When it comes to success, research shows that while IQ, education, and training play cameo roles, the starring role, the headliner on the success stage, is "Do you have a vision? Do you believe it's possible?"

Shawn Achor, author of *The Happiness Advantage*, calls it a "mental map." Much of reality, he says, is created not by outside facts, but by our own internal voices. If your mental map includes a deafening chorus of worry, anxiety, and fear, success rates plummet no matter how high on the Richter scale your smarts register.

Statistically, he claims that predicting success using any other factor (say, your IQ or number of degrees) is about as effective as flipping a coin.

What *is* effective, Achor and Frederickson and other happiness researchers have proven, is creating a happy brain that anticipates accomplishment, that knows success is just a matter of time.

Creating a neural net of positive expectation stacks the odds in your favor, giving you a 75 percent better chance of accomplishing your goals.

The Pudding

"In work and in life . . . we're supposed to have
so much fun, like puppy dogs with our tails wagging."
— DAVID LYNCH, FILMMAKER

Filmmaker David Lynch hasn't missed a day of meditating in more than 42 years. He says his Transcendental Meditation (TM) practice is the linchpin of everything he does, including diving deep into consciousness for film ideas that have won him numerous Oscar, Golden Globe, and Emmy nominations. But even more important, he says, is that meditation has dissolved what he calls "the suffocating rubber clown suit of negativity."

Before he began meditating, he says in his book *Catching the Big Fish*, "I was filled with anxieties and fears. I felt a sense of depression and anger." But by diving into the ocean of pure, vibrant consciousness that exists inside every human, he has found peace, joy, and bliss.

At first, he says, he had zero interest in meditation, thought it was a big, fat waste of time. But then he heard the phrase "true happiness lies within." That intrigued him enough to wonder, *Could meditation be the way to find "the happiness within"?*

At the exact moment he began asking questions about and researching various types of meditation, his sister called, told him she'd been practicing TM for six months. It was all he needed. In July 1973, he visited the Los Angeles TM center, met an instructor who looked like Doris Day, and began a journey that he describes as pure happiness—"not a goofball happiness, but a thick beauty."

I tell you this story not to sell you on the practice of Transcendental Meditation, but because it's a perfect demonstration of how we draw magnificence into our life once we decide to look for it, once we tune in to the gratitude channel.

Once we begin to want "true happiness," as Lynch did, the universe will send up flares.

Once you get on the gratitude frequency, you begin to notice there are burning bushes everywhere.

As Lynch says, "If you have a golf-ball-sized consciousness, you'll have a golf-ball-sized understanding . . . golf-ball-sized awareness . . . a golf-ball-sized inner happiness."

"The more your consciousness—your awareness—is expanded, the deeper you go toward this source, this thing that modern physics calls the Unified Field."

PARTY GAME #24

Laser Love to Everyone and Everything You See

"The truth is, we are all one connected thing."
— ELLEN DEGENERES, TALK-SHOW HOST

Today, you're going to treat everyone as if it's their birthday. Send molecules of love to everybody you see with your body's eyes and to every thought or memory of anybody that arises in your mind. Beam it, baby, right from your eyeballs.

Lasering good thoughts is a blessing you can give for free. To everybody. We're all energetically connected. One happy person can create many happy people.

#S&F
Let's see you fist bumping a stranger.

The Party Favor: Splash Around in Possibility

"What happens next is up to you."
— CHRIS SACCA, VENTURE CAPITALIST

"It's complicated."

This is one of the ego's biggest ploys. Making you think that being happy is complicated, convincing you that happiness is a frivolous waste of time.

Life, in fact, is really simple. It's just very, very, very different from what we've been taught.

Here's all you need to know:

Be in the moment. Don't judge. Love everything.

When you're on the right frequency, your life experience feels like play. There's no forcing. There's no wrong or right. You're just splashing around in possibility. The more childlike glee you feel, the more you can be sure it's coming from D-Buzz.

The Pudding

*"Time can be your bitch if you just
let go of the 'next' and the 'before.'"*

— AMY POEHLER, ACTRESS AND COMEDIAN

When we hang up the boxing gloves, fly the white flag of surrender, we discover that life has been rooting for us all along.

Michael Singer—whose monumental book *The Untethered Soul* taught us to look at our habitual thought patterns, to step back from what I call our crazy-uncle voices—is living proof that life is meant to be easy. Shockingly easy.

Once he began overriding the voices in his head, the voices we all listen to and think are us, life presented him with gift after gift that he never predicted or ever dreamed possible.

Once, while still a graduate student, he wrote a 30-page doctoral-level economic treatise without studying, without going to the library, without struggling in any way.

This was an important final paper that his fellow doctoral candidates were completely stressing about.

By that time, Singer had lost his desire to become an economics professor. He'd found a simpler, happier way of connecting with a deeper consciousness. The last thing he wanted to do was spend hours at the library, researching, poring over books. All he cared about was his deep meditation practice and this inner energy of peace and joy that was welling up inside of him.

Because he didn't give a flying Frisbee about his grade or whether or not he even finished the Ph.D., he completely released all mental and emotional pressures. He just let go and started writing. He filled notepad after notepad with a totally logical presentation that began with a premise, laid out an argument, and ended with a conclusion.

Not only did he receive an A, but the professor, who had already suggested that his rarely attending student call it quits, asked him to consider doing his dissertation under him.

Things like this became a regular occurrence. On another important exam, for which he had no interest in studying, he simple followed his guidance (once you let go of all the emotional crap, it's as clear as a plastic Dasani bottle) that led him to the class textbook, three different times to read one solitary page.

When the essays on the exam asked about the exact three topics he had been guided to read, he decided it was time to give it up for good. Not the Ph.D., but the idea that he needed to struggle or fight with life.

Singer, besides writing a rock star of a book, went on to buy 600 acres of pristine forest and meadows for a spiritual community, create a cutting-edge software package, and run a billion-dollar public company—all without any effort on his part. They were right there behind Door #1.

PARTY GAME #25

Spread Contagious Laughter

"Laughter is an instant vacation."

— MILTON BERLE, COMEDIAN AND ACTOR

Laugh today as often as possible.

If you have to, fake it. One year on my birthday, Taz and I went to an Adam Sandler movie. We decided beforehand to wage a contest to see who could produce the most styles of laughter. There's the snorting laugh, for example. And a quiet tee-hee titter. During any scene that was even remotely funny, we would let out some derivation of a guffaw. Before long, we were laughing so hard it became contagious. The entire theater was cracking up, and it wasn't just because of Sandler's histrionics.

People might think laughter is a ridiculous, trite, pointless goal, but it cured Norman Cousins of painful, life-threatening arthritis. And meditator Carlos Santana claims a good, gut-busting round of laughter is worth more than a month of sitting on the mat. Scientists say it decreases stress hormones, increases infection-fighting antibodies, and releases a whole medicine cabinet of feel-good chemicals. It sends oxygen to your tissues, increases your pulse and heart rate, and, according to Vanderbilt University researcher Maciej Buchowski, even burns calories.

The Web of Science database lists 6,447 published papers on the emotion of fear and only 175 on laughter, a sure giveaway of our culture values. Today be committed to this simple fact: You can't do both at the same time.

#S&F
Laughing, anyone?

The Party Favor: Ramp Up Your Consciousness

"I have chosen to be happy because it is good for my health."
— VOLTAIRE, PHILOSOPHER

After years of practicing traditional Western medicine, Dr. Amit Sood, professor at the Mayo Clinic College of Medicine, felt he was failing miserably at his doctorly goal of minimizing suffering.

In India, where he trained and practiced, it was easy to stop suffering. There, he treated serious illnesses and chronic problems like malnutrition. At Mayo, he noticed just as much suffering, but of a different kind.

"It didn't make sense to me," he said. "The emotional suffering here is out of control."

So he made a U-turn, went from internal medicine to what he calls "training people's minds for a better life."

Sood's patients (and this goes for 99.9 percent of us in the Western world) spend more than half their mental energy flitting from thought to thought without any real intentionality. This, he says, causes unnecessary suffering.

Now instead of prescribing medicine, he trains patients to be more intentional, to better choose where they deploy their attention.

Some might dismiss his simple "medicine" that restructures "neural predispositions"—except for one thing.

It actually works. Being thankful for every blessing, both large and small, has proven to be highly effective at dismantling the rut in which our brains operate.

As he says, "When I focus on my blessings, I feel full, and when I am full, I am ready to give and better able to withstand adversity."

The Pudding

> *"Stay close to any sounds*
> *That make you glad you are alive."*
>
> — HAFIZ, PERSIAN POET

Most of us take better care of our cars than we do of our thoughts. Emotions come and go—until we decide to build shrines to them.

In 2007, John Kralik, a California attorney, felt his life was going to hell. He'd gone through two divorces, his law firm was hemorrhaging money, and he was too embarrassed for his seven-year-old daughter to see the trash heap he was living in.

On New Year's Day, while walking in the woods, feeling like a complete loser, he heard a voice—a loud, clear voice that said, "Until you learn to be grateful for the things you have, you will not receive the things you want."

He had no idea who was talking to him. Was he going crazy? Was it an angel? Was it his grandfather who used to bug him about sending thank-you notes?

That the voice was coming from his dead grandfather seemed like the best alternative, and since he had little to lose, he decided to heed his grandpa's advice. He decided to spend 2008 writing thank-you notes.

His oldest son, the one from whom he'd been estranged, was first on the list. The letter prompted a lunch together, which prompted an amazing conversation, the best they'd had in years.

He then wrote notes to his Starbucks barista who always remembered his order, his building manager who had sent a plumber to fix his toilet. Then there were letters to clients, court clerks, real estate agents, and loan brokers. Then he started thanking people who'd made a difference to him when he was younger—a college friend, a surgeon who'd fixed his esophagus.

Almost immediately, significant and surprising benefits came his way—from financial gain to friendship, from weight loss to inner peace.

By December, Kralik says, "My life had improved so much I began to imagine a Hollywood ending. . . . My experience of [life], moment by moment, had been transformed. When bad things happened, they might slow me, but they no longer unraveled me. . . . The process of saying 'thank you' turned my life around and continues to do so to this moment."

PARTY GAME #26

Refuse to Talk Smack

*"The spiritual lens—even just the nightly gratitude list
and going over each day's actions—is starting to rewrite the story
of my life in the present, and I begin to feel like somebody
snatched out of the fire, salvaged, saved."*

— MARY KARR, AUTHOR OF *THE LIARS' CLUB*

Get your fear immunization. Do it for the home team.

Like a flu virus, fear and negativity is everywhere, looking for opportunities to invade. Unless it's treated quickly, it can spread from person to person. Don't be a carrier.

In this game, make a vow that for the next 24 hours, you will bring "all is well" to every table.

Gratitude is the formula for treating fear. You'll quickly find that fear and anxiety cannot exist at the same time as appreciation and contentment. If you repeat "thank you" over and over again, fear and misfortune will be eradicated.

#S&F
Show us you with someone you love.

The Party Favor: Gasp Out Loud

"Happiness . . . is the Holy Grail."

— SONJA LYUBOMIRSKY,
PSYCHOLOGY PROFESSOR AND HAPPINESS RESEARCHER

The Divine Buzz is the strongest frequency on planet Earth.

At all times, you're either plugged in, letting it have its way with you, or you're not and it can't. And if you're wondering if you have any reason to ask, I can honestly say, "Sorry. You will know."

There's no mistaking it. You feel giddy, excited, ready for anything. Your life automatically goes better. You have fascinating conversations. You notice people doing nice things for each other. Your body feels more flexible. Traffic lanes open up just for you. You know exactly how to deal with whatever happens to be in front of you. You don't have to figure it out ahead of time or plan. You simply trust that whatever is needed (an answer, an action, a word) will show up.

In sports, they call it "being in the zone."

You don't have to work at it. Or lure it in. Or be good enough to merit its attention. You just have to quit doubting its existence. And quit putting so much darned energy into its opposite.

The frequency (often called God) has absolutely nothing to do with saying the right prayers or joining the right religion or meditating the proper amount of minutes.

In fact, I rarely use the word *God*, that, to my way of thinking, has more baggage than a Delta cargo hold. In my books, I've borrowed a physics term and called it the *field of infinite potentiality*—the FP, for short. I've also been known to call it the Divine Buzz the Universe, or Radiant X. I think it's good to mix it up a bit, to keep it fresh and relevant. God doesn't fit in a box. God is the very energy of life, a frequency that never stops broadcasting.

It's always present, always here to interact with us, guide us, bless us.

Our only job is to become a better receiving station—and, hopefully, transmit the signal to surrounding pessimists.

The Pudding

> *"We lived in that web of magic, connected by the*
> *silver filaments of chance and circumstance."*
>
> — ROBERT MCCAMMON, AUTHOR OF *BOY'S LIFE*

When Carlos Santana was 15, his family moved from Baja California to San Francisco. He wasn't crazy about the idea, particularly since he was already supporting himself playing strip joints and clubs in downtown Tijuana. After a big blowup with his mom, he announced that he was heading back to Mexico. He would catch a ride with some of his father's friends.

As soon as he pulled into town, he went straight to Our Lady of Guadalupe, the big cathedral downtown. He kneeled at the altar and said to the Virgin, "I want you to help my family be safe where they are. And help me get a job tonight. That's all I want."

He went straight from the church to El Convoy, the club where he used to play. The manager walked up to him as if he'd seen a ghost, "I'm sorry. You can't be here. Your mom told us she was taking you to America. And because you're underage, we can't let you play here without your parents' permission."

Carlos reached into his pocket and handed him a handwritten letter from his mom, a letter he didn't know was there, a letter that magically appeared just when he needed it.

His mother swore until her dying day that she didn't write it. She'd get furious every time Carlos brought it up.

How did it get there? Carlos has no idea.

But either way, the manager shrugged, pointed at the stage, and said, "Go ahead, get up there. And welcome back."

PARTY GAME #27

The Jimmy Fallon Game

*"My life is a party, to be experienced
and shared with everyone I know!"*

— LOUISE HAY, AUTHOR AND FOUNDER OF HAY HOUSE

Approach today with the boyish enthusiasm and puppy-eyed fascination of Jimmy Fallon.

View your life and everything in it as a surprise party staged just for you. Suck up to everyone you meet. You'll find as you treat everyone like Fallon treats the celebs on his show that your interactions will be relaxed, loose, and pressure-free. While you're at it, giggle like a teenager; engage in shenanigans; and challenge friends to dance-offs, lip-sync battles, or makeshift *Family Feud*'s.

'Course if you're not convinced that relentless, joyous silliness is a good way to spend a day, take it from the Greek philosophers, who were very clear that wonder and astonishment are the doorway to wisdom, the entry into the consciousness that animates all things.

#S&F
Let's see your "after" picture because,
after all, who cares about before?

The Party Favor: Supplement Conventional Medicine

"Gratitude is like a magnet; the more grateful you are, the more you will receive to be grateful for."

— IYANLA VANZANT,
LAWYER AND NEW THOUGHT SPIRITUAL TEACHER

If you're not getting personal signs and blessings from the universe, you're not paying attention. Or . . . you're convinced that (and therefore creating a reality where) interaction with a higher Source is improbable and highly unlikely. Maybe you consider it strictly the province of mumbling guys with no teeth.

Personally, I wouldn't have it any other way. Even though I'm educated and consider myself an intelligent, rational person, I'm perfectly okay with being lumped in with the toothless mumblers. In fact, getting and noticing personal signs and blessings from the Dude, as I call the Bigger Thing in *E-Squared*, and sharing with friends about their signs and blessings is my number one hobby. As I frequently say, it's the only conversation that really matters.

The rest no longer makes sense to me.

To satisfy my penchant for magic and miracles, I belong to a couple of what I call my "possibility posses" (one of which I mentioned back in Party Game #6). These groups get together several times a month to talk possibility, quantum physics, and the miraculous world we choose to see.

Let me repeat those words—*choose* to look for and register magic. That is our intention, our sole purpose. We're a support group, I guess you could say, for warding off the more prevalent story of lack and limitation.

Some of us even go so far as to talk to angels and place their advice above the columnists in the newspaper who would direct us to worry.

Here's one such story shared by my possibility posse pal Bettie:

After months of severe pain in her right bicep, Bettie consulted with the medical community. Four different doctors, all of whom conducted numerous tests, came up with the same (non-)diagnosis: "There's clearly inflammation and pain, but tests are show nada, zilch."

It made no sense.

Bettie, feeling discouraged, walked out of the last doctor's office and noticed a penny on the ground. Whenever she finds a penny, she considers it a wink from her angels. She looked up, said "thanks," picked it up, and put it in her pants pocket.

Next morning, her partner looked at her, alarmed.

"What in the heck? There's something really weird on the back of your neck.'

Upon further examination, they found the "weird growth" was actually the penny Bettie had deposited in her pocket the day before, now stuck to the back of her neck. During the night, the "angel penny" had literally adhered to her skin above her C6 vertebra. When Bettie returned to the doctor and asked them to check her C6 vertebra, they found a bone spur that—ask any chiropractor—controls the wrist extensors and provides innervation to the bicep. Once the spur was removed, the pain completely disappeared.

The Pudding

> *"The secret to life is always listen to your music*
> *in the car really loud with the windows down."*
>
> — LESLIE BUTSCH,
> SOCIAL WORKER IN LAWRENCE, KANSAS

Another posse mate, Robbin, is a sponsor for a Unity Church youth group. At a regional conference, she logged so many miles in preparation that she developed a limp. Her feet, as we mistakenly say, were "killing" her.

Cursory treatments from a nurse and an energy healer provided no relief. Robbin continued to limp around.

The first night of the conference, the energetic high school students started to dance. Robbin, watching with great glee from the sidelines, could no longer resist. She leaped into the fray, dancing with wild abandon.

Suddenly, it occurred to her: *My foot is fine. I'm healed.*

Moral of this story is that as long as we look for healing (indicating a belief that healing is necessary), we put energy into the problem. But once we withdraw energy from the "problem," it's free to disappear.

Divine Playfulness

> *"Devote a slice of your energies towards*
> *making the world suck less every week."*
>
> — SHONDA RHIMES, CREATOR OF *GREY'S ANATOMY*
> AND LOTS OF OTHER TELEVISION SHOWS

What love mischief can you get into this fine and glorious day?

- Smuggle a bar of soap into a restaurant or bar; use it to write encouraging comments on the bathroom mirrors, things like "You are so beautiful," "Never forget you are loved," "Your life makes a difference."

- Go caroling in July. Whether or not you sing "We wish you a merry Christmas" is up to you.

- Make up business-sized cards that say, "You have uplifted and inspired me today. Thank you." Pass them out liberally.

- Add mirth to public bulletin boards. My friend Annola once made a poster that said TAKE WHAT YOU NEED. On each strip at the bottom, the ones that normally list phone numbers, she wrote *peace, love, contentment, happiness.* The strips were gone by lunchtime.

- Take selfies with your neighbors. I know. You haven't talked to your neighbor to the west since her dog left the mess in your leaf pile. But these are your closest comrades in the game of life. Get to know them.

- While you're at it, take selfies with as many strangers as you can. Ask them "What's your favorite thing to do?" and "What's your vision for the world?"

- Host a show-and-tell party. Why isn't this a normal thing? Every week or so we should get together with family and friends and show them something we really like, something unique. Bring in some doodle we made on the side of a Visa bill or something we thought up while waiting at the dry cleaner's. Adults still think things up. We just don't tell anyone. We don't think it's important. Not with lawns that need mowing and mufflers that need fixing.

- Get everybody on the subway or at the bus stop to sing "Over the Rainbow." For inspiration, check out Peter Sharp, a fabulous Aussie who calls himself a social artist and world peacemaker (www.petersharp.com.au). His YouTube videos are better mood lifters than Prozac. Sharp has led public happiness experiments (he calls them shock waves of inspiration) in Barcelona, Perth, and London, to name a few. As he says, if the world is going to change, it needs to start with normal people who give a damn.

- Wear a weird costume. Carry a large stuffed animal. Do something that makes people point and smile.

- Host a gratitude circle.

- Stage a public dance party. I recently wrote a story for *People* magazine about Gary Logan, an assistant principal in Conway, Arkansas, who leads grade schoolers in the cha-cha every Friday. The gregarious administrator welcomes his students each with a song and a dance. The kids can't wait to get to school; they bug their parents: "C'mon, c'mon, we gotta get there." Logan, who says he never has a bad day, gets to school at 7:05 every morning and leads his charges in line dances, the Whip/Nae Nae. "We've found that if the kids get out their wiggles and the giggles, they're ready to settle down into school," Logan says.

Your Closing Thank & Grow Rich Earnings Report

So, my friend, how did you do? Let's take another look at your Thank & Grow Rich portfolio. Again, using the criteria listed in Chapter 5, let's chart your performance on a scale of 1 to 10.

TODAY'S DATE: _____

LOVE
80.9 + 5.6 (6.92%)

ROI (RETURN ON INVESTMENT)

ALCHEMIC CAPITAL:	1 2 3 4 5 6 7 8 9 10
SPIRITUAL CAPITAL:	1 2 3 4 5 6 7 8 9 10
CREATIVE CAPITAL:	1 2 3 4 5 6 7 8 9 10
SOCIAL CAPITAL:	1 2 3 4 5 6 7 8 9 10
ADVENTURE CAPITAL:	1 2 3 4 5 6 7 8 9 10

CAPITAL GAINS (AKA GIFT TRACKING)

PERSONAL TOTEM OR SYMBOL: _____

BLESSINGS FROM NATURAL WORLD: _____

MESSAGE FROM OTHER SIDE: _____

SHATTERED ABSOLUTE FACT: _____

AFTERWORD

*"We did not come all this great distance, and
make all this great effort, only to miss the party."*
— ELIZABETH GILBERT, AUTHOR OF *BIG MAGIC*

If you've gotten this far, we might as well make it official. You're now a bona fide member of the Truth and Merriment League.

Please raise your hand and proclaim:

*I hereby acknowledge that I am here on planet Earth to extend
love . . . that I'm here at this unique time-space reality to create the good, the holy, and the beautiful. And I commit to live
this sacred Truth from this moment forward.*

Now that we've gotten that out of the way, it's time to can the old "What's it all about?" shtick you've been harping on for the last 30, 40 years.

You are here to expand the universe. And it's as easy as your next thought.

Although I won't be sending out any secret decoder rings, the party games in this book can accomplish the same thing. They're intended to raise your vibration, help you move away from the old story. And they don't have to be played exclusively within the confines of the book's 30-day experiment. Anytime you notice your frequency wavering, open up Part III, randomly point to a page, take a deep breath, and proclaim, "Wahoo, baby!

As you step out of the phone booth, there are a couple . . . let's just call them habits . . . that you might as well leave behind next to Clark Kent's glasses and wing tips.

Moving away from these bad habits will make your odyssey going forward a lot easier.

1. **Quit being a seeker.** You don't need another book, another seminar, another practice. *You got this!* It's etched into your DNA. One of the reasons you haven't yet claimed your power to expand the universe is because you've been too busy trying to find it in all this self-help crap. I'm not pointing fingers. I've been doing it, too. I have contributed to the pocketbooks of thousands of self-help authors. But that era is so yesterday. Now is the time to claim our inheritance, to rule our kingdom, to become the wise, loving creators we buried underneath all the how-to books.

2. **Ditch the seriousness.** Being a universe expander is a game. A really frickin' fun game. Some might say it's a sonic blast. The only way to properly approach your new role is with great joy and glee. Enough of this seven steps to enlightenment. Begone all weighty requirements. See above rejoinder: *You got this.* Repeat hourly.

3. **Laugh in the face of the Debbie Downers.** Probably the most insidious bad habit, the Molasses Swamp (remember *Candy Land?*) we've all fallen into, is using our superpowers to create fear. Our beliefs and expectations are the Play-Doh that form the world we see. But instead of using them to dream up new and astounding possibilities, we use them like nuclear bombs, wiping out entire lifetimes with one misaligned detonation. Rather

than use them to imagine new things, to create a world that works for all of us, we rinse and repeat the same stuff we've been hearing for generations. Someday we'll look back and laugh at the lengths to which we misused our powers. We'll read the history books regaling our beliefs in separation and limits and wonder, *Really? Are you kidding me? Why would anyone choose to suffer when right at their fingertips is the power to create a beautiful, engaging, completely cool reality?*

4. Loosen your grip on the reins and realize it's not you. You're just a conduit. You don't have to do a damned thing. In fact, the less you get involved, the better the outcome is sure to be. This, of course, involves faith. And a rewiring of your brain.

~⌇~

And lastly, if anybody asks what *Thank & Grow Rich* is all about, remind them of this:

- We are here at this remarkable time on planet Earth to expand the universe, not to win Academy Awards for how talented we are at suffering.

- Ordinary daily life is the most perfect ashram for finding peace, contentment, and the Divine Buzz.

- One of the greatest ways we can serve our fellow travelers is to figure out a way to enjoy ourselves and to let people know that enjoying themselves is a good thing.

And then tell them to meet you at _____ on _____ for a weekly celebration of happiness amplification. No pathological reruns of yesterday allowed. Training yourself to see goodness and value in everything is an insanely radical notion.

That's why it's so imperative to do this high-vibe business with others who (a) are committed to bringing their best game, (b) know the only thing worth talking about is what's working, and (c) know that we are *all* beautiful lights with beautiful ideas to change the world.

Remember, if you do what makes you happy, it gives the rest of us permission to be happy.

Oh, and One More Thing

Don't forget, you're invited to the revolution currently happening at the Thank & Grow Rich town hall on Instagram and Facebook. Go team!

Instagram.com/thankandgrowrich/
#T&GRtotem
#T&GRnaturalbling
#T&GRmessage
#T&GRshatteredfact

In lieu of tattooing their names upon my body—aka:

ACKNOWLEDGMENTS

"May peace be your ellipsis and joy your exclamation point."
— CHRISTINE SMITH,
ONE OF MY TUESDAY NIGHT *SCRABBLE* BUDDIES

As you can imagine, a book on gratitude is destined to have a ton of peeps to thank. I considered a companion volume just so I could list the name of every single person who I now owe a double tall macchiato.

But, as my high school journalism professor taught me, keep it brief, concise, and to the point. And if you can't, at least make sure it fits on one page.

So . . .

I'd like to start by giving a shout-out to all the fun, funky coffee shops in Lawrence, Kansas, where I wrote nearly all the games in the Truth and Merriment League Game and Toy Box. As I once heard Robert Holden say, "Caffeine is the Holy Spirit's delivery system."

Hats off to Cheryl Miller, who also fueled and fed me at her Fairchild Wellness Center in Overbrook, Kansas, at various key stages during the writing of this book.

As for spiritual food, I acknowledge the beautiful words of Hafiz and Rumi and of Charles Eisenstein, Ethan

Hughes, Tom Shadyac, and Nipun Mehta, who are already modeling the gift economy I so revere.

As usual, I owe the moon and the Big Dipper to my possibility posses, whose members make up a large portion of these pages. Mad props to each and every one of you:

Rhonda Burgess, Jay Pryor, Annola Charity, Linda Gwaltney, Carla Mumma, Elizabeth Stiers, Diane Silver, Robbin Loomas, Cheryl Miller, Melanie Black Loyd, Frank Schwaller, Jan Spiegel, Kris Hicks, Pat Weaver, Ronn Gifford, Kitty Tootles, Nikki Wright, Jennie Washburn, K. C. Bushnell, Bettie Wilson, Cindy McCracken, Joyce Barrett, M. K. Mueller, Bonita Yoder, and even Buddy F*#-ing Biancalana, the famous World Series baseball player who showed up one Sunday, proving that some manifestations take longer than others.

Deep bows and open hearts forever to the home team, without whom I couldn't function: Jim Dick; the whole Sheridan clan; and, as always, my incredible daughter, Tasman McKay Grout, who, above all else, keeps me humble.

I salute the entirety of Hay House, especially Alex Freemon, who put up with my bullheadedness; Melissa Brinkerhoff, who generously sends my books to everyone from maximum-security prisoners in Nashville to wide-eyed teenagers in South Africa; the ever-patient Christy Salinas; Lisa Cheng; and Patty Gift.

Last but not least, I trumpet my thanks to my growing posse of full-moon dancers who, individually or together, gather wherever they might be to dance to the full moon in joyous celebration of this fierce and mystical planet we all inhabit together.

ABOUT THE AUTHOR

Pam Grout is an explorer on the frontiers of magic and enchantment. She has served as an extra in a zombie movie; composed a country-and-western song; created a TV series; and communed with Maasai warriors, Turkish sultans, and Inti the Ecuadorian Sun God. For a living (and she always wonders why that's most people's number one question), she writes books (18, at last count, including the international bestseller *E-Squared: 9 Do-It-Yourself Energy Experiments That Prove Your Thoughts Create Your Reality*) and articles for such places as CNN Travel, *Men's Journal*, *The Huffington Post*, and *People* magazine. She can be tracked down at www.pamgrout.com, @PamGrout, and Facebook.com/pam.grout.fanpage.

Hay House Titles of Related Interest

YOU CAN HEAL YOUR LIFE, the movie,
starring Louise Hay & Friends
(available as a 1-DVD program and an expanded 2-DVD set)
Watch the trailer at: www.LouiseHayMovie.com

THE SHIFT, the movie, starring Dr. Wayne W. Dyer
(available as a 1-DVD program and an expanded 2-DVD set)
Watch the trailer at: www.DyerMovie.com

ASK AND IT IS GIVEN: *Learning to Manifest Your Desires,*
by Esther and Jerry Hicks

SHIFT HAPPENS!: *How to Live an Inspired Life . . .
Starting Right Now!,* by Robert Holden

THE POWER OF NO: *Because One Little
Word Can Bring Health, Abundance, and Happiness,*
by James Altucher and Claudia Azula Altucher

THE INSIDE-OUT REVOLUTION: *The Only Thing You Need
to Know to Change Your Life Forever,* by Michael Neill

DYING TO BE ME: *My Journey from Cancer,
to Near Death, to True Healing,* by Anita Moorjani

TRUST: *Mastering the 4 Essential Trusts: Trust in Self, Trust in
God, Trust in Others, FjokTrust in Life,* by Iyanla Vanzant

LIFE'S OPERATING MANUAL:
With the Fear and Truth Dialogues, by Tom Shadyac

YOU CAN CREATE AN EXCEPTIONAL LIFE,
by Louise Hay and Cheryl RIchardson

All of the above are available at your local bookstore,
or may be ordered by contacting Hay House (see next page).

We hope you enjoyed this Hay House book. If you'd like to receive
our online catalog featuring additional information on Hay House books
and products, or if you'd like to find out more about the
Hay Foundation, please contact:

Hay House, Inc., P.O. Box 5100, Carlsbad, CA 92018-5100
(760) 431-7695 or (800) 654-5126
(760) 431-6948 (fax) or (800) 650-5115 (fax)
www.hayhouse.com® • www.hayfoundation.org

Published and distributed in Australia by:
Hay House Australia Pty. Ltd., 18/36 Ralph St., Alexandria NSW 2015
Phone: 612-9669-4299 • *Fax:* 612-9669-4144 • www.hayhouse.com.au

Published and distributed in the United Kingdom by: Hay House UK, Ltd.,
Astley House, 33 Notting Hill Gate, London W11 3JQ
Phone: 44-20-3675-2450 • *Fax:* 44-20-3675-2451 • www.hayhouse.co.uk

Published and distributed in the Republic of South Africa by:
Hay House SA (Pty), Ltd., P.O. Box 990, Witkoppen 2068
info@ hayhouse.co.za • www.hayhouse.co.za

Published in India by: Hay House Publishers India,
Muskaan Complex, Plot No. 3, B-2, Vasant Kunj, New Delhi 110 070
Phone: 91-11-4176-1620 • *Fax:* 91-11-4176-1630 • www.hayhouse.co.in

Distributed in Canada by: Raincoast Books,
2440 Viking Way, Richmond, B.C. V6V 1N2 •
Phone: 1-800-663-5714 • *Fax:* 1-800-565-3770 • www.raincoast.com

<u>**Take Your Soul on a Vacation**</u>

Visit www.HealYourLife.com® to regroup, recharge,
and reconnect with your own magnificence.
Featuring blogs, mind-body-spirit news, and
life-changing wisdom from Louise Hay and friends.
Visit www.HealYourLife.com today!

Free e-newsletters from Hay House, the Ultimate Resource for Inspiration

Be the first to know about Hay House's dollar deals, free downloads, special offers, affirmation cards, giveaways, contests, and more!

 Get exclusive excerpts from our latest releases and videos from *Hay House Present Moments*.

 Enjoy uplifting personal stories, how-to articles, and healing advice, along with videos and empowering quotes, within *Heal Your Life*.

 Have an inspirational story to tell and a passion for writing? Sharpen your writing skills with insider tips from *Your Writing Life*.

Sign Up Now!

Get inspired, educate yourself, get a complimentary gift, and share the wisdom!

http://www.hayhouse.com/newsletters.php

Visit www.hayhouse.com to sign up today!

  HealYourLife.com ♥